THE
LIBERATING
LAW

THE LIBERATING LAW

BY

GERARD REED

An Adaptation for Discussion

EVERETT LEADINGHAM, EDITOR

Though this book is designed for group study, it is also intended for personal enjoyment and spiritual growth. A leader's guide is available from your local bookstore or your publisher.

Beacon Hill Press of Kansas City
Kansas City, Missouri

Editor: Everett Leadingham

Assistant Editor: Charlie L. Yourdon

Executive Editor: Randy Cloud

Editorial Committee: Philip Baisley, Carolyn Clements, Randy Cloud, David Higle, Everett Leadingham, Thomas Mayse, Larry Morris, Charlie L. Yourdon

Cover design: Paul Franitza

10   9   8   7   6   5   4   3   2   1

CONTENTS

Chapter 1	Wanted: Some Imperatives!	7
Chapter 2	The Covenant Context: God Is Present	17
Chapter 3	The Promise Perfected: A New Covenant	29
Chapter 4	A Sacred Trust	36
Chapter 5	A Sacrosanct Focus	44
Chapter 6	A Hallowed Name Above All Names	54
Chapter 7	A Sanctified Cosmos	63
Chapter 8	The Sanctity of the Family	73
Chapter 9	The Sanctity of Life	84
Chapter 10	The Sanctity of Sex	95
Chapter 11	The Sanctity of Property	104
Chapter 12	The Sanctity of Our Word	115
Chapter 13	The Sanctity of Satisfaction	125

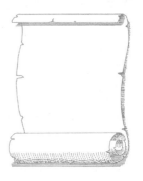

Background Scripture:
Matthew 19:16-17;
Galatians 5:6; 6:2;
James 1:25

CHAPTER 1

WANTED: SOME IMPERATIVES!

"LET'S FACE IT," SAYS ANN LANDERS, "[Our culture] is sick."[1] The sickness whereof she speaks is a plague of immorality. From the urbane white-collar con artists to urban teenagers "wilding" and "tagging," something has subverted our morality. Yet exactly what has happened is generally more confused than clarified by television, newspapers, or congressional hearings.

An ancient explanation rooted in the Christian tradition claims that our sickness stems from failing to know the truth of our own moral nature. Embedded in human nature is an abiding reality—an ethical vein. Doing right, we live according to its structure; doing wrong, we violate its essence. We humans share a common nature: living creatures designed in God's image and likeness, animated by our Creator, coded to live out His standards. So living rightly requires religious roots. Forsaking the vision of our divinely designed character, we forgo the capacity to do good. Religion as the source of morality has been replaced with personal feelings and societal programs.

One of the keys to understanding what has happened resides in the values that emerged in the 1960s, a decade that was devoted to "little else but sex and rights—specifically, how to get more of each."[2] Since then, we've been swept along by an avalanche of collapsing moral standards. In some ways this process is best illustrated by the sexual behavior of a man named Gaetan Dugas, the airline steward who played a prominent role in spreading AIDS. In the decade before the disease became an epidemic, Dugas averaged 250 sexual encounters a year. In his words, "It's my right to do what I want with my body."[3] His "right," of course, cost him his life and lethally infected thousands of others. Individuals who insist on their rights rather than assuming the obligation to do right grease the cultural slide into a moral quagmire.

Sociological data illustrate such moral anarchy. *The Day America Told the Truth,* a portrayal based upon extensive interviews, profiles a woman who worked as a prostitute for two years and is now married. One of her daughters, she suspects, was fathered by a man other than her husband—though neither her husband nor her daughter suspect this. The woman is unhappy with her marriage, uses drugs, admits she is bulimic, and has considered suicide.

She does, however, consider herself a "good, ethical person. On a ten-point scale from 'terrible' to 'great,' she gives herself a nine. She is religious, a frequent churchgoer, absolutely certain of God's existence."[4] She no doubt believes in a God who loves her unconditionally, too gracious to hold her accountable before any bar of justice.

This woman illustrates the findings of a survey that reveals only one out of every three "Christians" believes faith should shape his or her lifestyle! Believe that God accepts us just as we are, accept the fact that we are accepted, and then do whatever is acceptable to us! Professed believers feel free to construct their own morality, removing the

Ten Commandments from the walls of their hearts as well as the halls of our public buildings.

No wonder onlookers scoff at so-called Christians! Too many "believers" are like chubby physicians who tell their patients to lose weight. If the Christian Church is to recover its integrity, we Christians must reclaim and proclaim some timeless truths, some moral imperatives, and walk rightly with God.

This issue, in a philosophical sense, stands revealed in Allan Bloom's book *The Closing of the American Mind*. Today's students, Bloom says, are nice enough, even if unusually self-centered. Disinterested in human nature and lacking curiosity about philosophical themes such as God, freedom, and immortality, today's youngsters think mainly about their own feelings and frustrations. They want to "discover themselves."

Without objective standards, Bloom believes, we're awash in a pervasive ethical relativism. Under the flags of "openness" and "tolerance" (while tolerating no universal truths or traditional values), folks freely follow their own feelings.[5] As a Hemingway character contended, "Morality is in the eye of the beholder. So far, about morals, I know only that what is moral is what you feel good after and what is immoral is what you feel bad after."[6]

Such moral permissiveness, many believe, constitutes a free and democratic society. To probe deeply into the reasons for this, Bloom digs for the philosophical roots of today's malaise and finds "nihilism, American style"—the "attempt to get beyond good and evil" by substituting "value relativism" for Judeo-Christian absolutism.[7]

Bloom's critique finds support in a speech given by Michael Novak. "One principle that today's intellectuals most passionately disseminate is vulgar relativism. . . . For them . . . there is no truth, only opinion: my opinion, your opinion." Consequently, "The most perilous threat to the free society today is neither political nor economic. It is the poisonous, corrupting culture of relativism."[8]

Given this threat, Christ's Church must recover a moral source higher than opinion polls and momentary personal feelings. It makes no more sense to consult public opinion on moral questions than it would to hold an election to determine the size of the highest peak in the Rocky Mountains. Moral standards resemble mountain ranges—they're majestically there, they're measurable, they have an arched pattern, and we ignore the unyielding absoluteness of their nature to our own discomfort or destruction. So we must intentionally point out and teach moral standards. This means pastors, parents, and teachers must reclaim their rightful responsibilities, wresting them from television talk shows, movie stars, politicians, and street gangs. It's time, in short, to recover and proclaim traditional Judeo-Christian moral standards!

At the heart of this crisis, as Aleksandr Solzhenitsyn saw, is this: "Men have forgotten God."[9] Everywhere, it seems, there's a great vacuum regarding supernatural reality. By nature, humans crave a "Holy Other," an ultimate reason for being that gives the present meaning and direction. When God is shoved aside, conscience evaporates and anarchy ensues.

Fortunately for us still rooted in the Christian tradition, there are some absolutes, some imperatives that have stood the test of time. The list was etched in stone, embedded in the Ten Commandments—10 rules to live by; 10 words to guide us; 10 ways to sustain a lasting, loving relationship with our Creator. Indeed, in the Jewish tradition, the day the commandments were given on Mount Sinai was often portrayed as a wedding day—a momentous event when binding vows were exchanged between two parties, which cemented a loving union. They are 10 steps to freedom, for, as the psalmist rejoiced, "I will walk about in freedom, for I have sought out your precepts" (Psalm 119:45).

Boundaries Create Freedom's Context

With the 10 words in Exodus 20, the God who had delivered His people from slavery set forth principles whereby folks live in relationship with Him. To know God is to enjoy the freedom that grows out of faithfulness, and this is the only true liberty there is, the freedom that comes from living by vows. Real freedom emerges through self-discipline and integrity, through doing the truth, through living in the truth.

Eight times in Exodus 20 the Lord begins a statement with "You shall." Here we hear a commanding voice. He also said "Remember" and "Honor," two more imperative verbs. Some things, He made clear, we must do to maintain faithfulness with Him. There are limits to healthy, holy living.

All good things have boundaries. Our bodies, for example, have bone boundaries. Were there no restraints on the molecules of my bones, if every individual cell did its own thing, slipping and sliding wherever it pleased, I'd be a glob of jelly, unable to walk or hold hands with my wife. I'm free to move, free to experience the joys of life, because my bones have hard-and-fast boundaries, hard-and-fast edges.

My skin as well is a restraining boundary, a definable limit to my body, keeping out what would injure me, keeping in what is vital for me. I'm able to live freely because my skin keeps me together, firmly, in the place where I ought to be.

So, too, social and personal boundaries are necessary for the good life. Increasingly, it seems, what was once disgraceful now elicits little condemnation. A rabbi asks an important question with the title of his book, *Doesn't Anyone Blush Anymore?*[10] Some of us wonder today if there's anything truly off-limits or inappropriate. Are there real boundaries?

In truth, there are boundaries acknowledged by healthy men and women. If we're morally mature persons, we see how things are, and act accordingly, doing the truth. The boundaries are there for us to discover as responsible persons. Good relationships need boundaries, limits, dos and don'ts.

Responsibilities Firm Up the Boundaries

When we accept responsibilities, we firm up the boundaries needed for good relationships, for a good life. This stands out clearly in an essay that was written by a college senior and appeared in *Newsweek*. He listed his laments, a series of complaints against his elders. He admitted that this generation of collegians have poor Scholastic Aptitude Test (SAT) scores, know little geography or foreign languages, read very little, and are prisoners of fashionable fads. Yet, he claimed, "You did this to us. You prized your youth so much you made sure ours would be carefree." Parents loved their children, urging them to succeed and be happy, but they failed to teach them "to be responsible."[11]

This illustrates what John Rosemond, a psychologist, predicted years ago when he spoke out against the so-called experts in his profession who were "promoting the entirely ludicrous idea that happiness and self-esteem go hand in hand." In fact, "Self-esteem and happiness are not one and the same. Keeping a child happy is as simple as giving the child everything he or she wants. That may prove expensive, but it's not difficult. Keeping a child happy takes less effort, less stamina, and certainly less courage than helping a child to grow up."

If parents keep a child "happy" for 18 years, Rosemond asserted, they will "completely destroy the child's self-esteem. Self-esteem is composed of equal parts initiative, resourcefulness, imagination, autonomy, and determination." When parents fail to insist that children accept responsibility, when they try to keep them "happy" all the time, they keep them from growing up. "When the time comes for these children to leave home and begin fending for themselves, many of them will not be prepared for self-sufficiency."[12]

The key to personal dignity is the self-sufficiency that comes through taking responsibility, through accepting and carrying through obligations—in short, through self-discipline. To live well, to live maturely, to live freely demands self-discipline. Others may force us to do right, but only self-discipline, freely embraced, enables us to be righteous, to be good. Ultimately, self-discipline is moral—doing what's right because it's good.

I could pour a gallon of gasoline on the ground at the service station and light it (assuming no one stopped me), but it would just create a brief blazing bonfire. Only when I put it into my gas tank, routing it to my car's engine, where it explodes under tight restraints, does it serve my need for transportation. Only contained, restricted, disciplined explosions of gasoline do productive work.

Relationships Demand the Limits of Self-discipline

That, really, is what the Ten Commandments are all about. They are not endless rules with penalties for failure; they're 10 principles to live by. Ten ways to maintain fellowship with God. Ten words to be kept so as to behold His manifest presence. Ten boundaries to respect in order to nurture a loving union with our Maker. They are 10 steps to freedom!

Note that no threats accompany the commandments. God didn't say, "You shall not make graven images, because if you do, the next day a locomotive-sized meteorite will annihilate you." He didn't say, "You shall not commit adultery, for if you do, the next morning you'll be reduced to a glob of putty." No, He just spoke 10 words—a recipe for living rightly with Him.

The Ten Commandments are a bit like guidelines for courteous courting. The only good reason for courting is to develop a good relationship with another person. Now I know some folks date for the wrong reasons—sexual thrills, ego satisfactions, free food. But those are just perversions of the only good reason for dating—to get to know another person.

Consequently, healthy dates have definable limits. A single person, if wise, doesn't try to date two people at the same time. What's true for dating is equally true for marriage. A couple out for a stroll do not continually inspect and favorably comment on the attributes of every other person they pass. There are limits to how much they can notice others, to how much they can admire others, when they're in a loving relationship.

It's obvious: self-discipline (restricting ourselves to one person) establishes what we most long for—a loving relationship, a lasting union with a person. So, just as there are limits we must respect in courtships that mature into loving bonds, there are limits we must revere if we sustain any bond with God.

Rightly understood, God's commandments are not narrow restrictions meant to cramp our style. They are liberating steps, guiding us to the self-discipline basic to any lasting, loving relationship with God. The Lord seeks to draw us into a covenant bond, a lasting union, a spiritual marriage with himself.

We who want to live with God have clear guidelines for doing right—the Ten Commandments. We need to grow up, to accept the freedom God has given us, and to take responsibility for our actions. We must remember, however, that these commandments were given us as ways whereby we complete a covenant, not as edicts arbitrarily imposed to exact obedience. So it's important, before turning to the specifics of the Bible's legal code, to consider its context. Only in covenant can the law be truly fulfilled. Only in covenant is the law fully liberating. And only in the new covenant, consummated by Christ Jesus, is the law truly liberating.

Such covenant theology underlies God's call to holy living. It sums up the Bible's call to holiness, personified in Jesus, incarnate Truth. In Christ, we discover our calling to freedom in obedience to the divine law summarized in the commandment of love of God and neighbor. This is what takes place through the gift of the Holy Spirit: in Him we are enabled to internalize the law, to receive it, and to live it as the motivating force of true personal freedom, "the perfect law, the law of liberty" (James 1:25, RSV).[13]

Jesus is the Light of the World. We who follow Him walk in the light and, by obeying His Word, live holy lives. Consequently, as we wonder how to decide what's right and wrong, what's good and bad, we discover that Jesus Christ is the answer to all of humanity's deepest hunger for truth. Thus, the Gospel account of the rich young man who came to Jesus illuminates the entire human condition. The young man asked, "Teacher, what good thing must I do to get eternal life?" (Matthew 19:16). All of us ask that question, a fundamentally moral question, which implicitly wonders about life's purpose, our final end.

Responding to the young man, Jesus reminded him that "there is only One who is good" (v. 17), God himself. Revering and serving God precedes all morality. Then we rightly obey His edicts—both the commandments inscribed in the natural law and the divine law revealed on Mount Sinai. To that, we add the righteous attitudes and motives prescribed in the Beatitudes, which enable one to follow Christ, who gives meaning to Christian ethics.

Through the grace given us as believers, the presence of the Holy Spirit enables us to live conformed to Christ's likeness. Law and grace work together. "Faith expressing itself through love" (Galatians 5:6) is the central formula, for it enables us to "fulfill the law of Christ" (6:2). There's an interaction to the Christlike life. Faith is more than mental assent. It's a commitment, a devotion to a loving relationship with God through Christ, who is the Way, the

Truth, and the Life. This faith, totally trusting Him, opens our hearts to His love, which in turn enables us to love Him and our neighbor.

When we try to live under the law, we seek comfort in grace; and with grace we find strength to live out the law. Saved by grace through faith, we're enabled by the Holy Spirit to live out the new law, which enfleshes in our hearts the statutes of Sinai.

Christ's Church, therefore, has one compelling commission—to bring persons to Jesus. By preaching the gospel, by bringing sinners to salvation, by affording them means of grace, the Church gives persons the opportunity—the birthright of believers—to live righteously. The high standards of morality are for Christians, men and women willingly transformed by the supernatural workings of God's grace. Such is possible only for persons free to choose, so freedom must be treasured in order for morality to exist. It is in fact possible to live rightly, for God does not command us to do what we cannot do.

Consequently, there are various behaviors that are clearly right and others that are manifestly wrong. Just as there are clearly defined rules in a game of baseball, there is an objective reality to moral acts that makes them intrinsically right or wrong. This eliminates various personal opinions and calculating ethical judgments, for Christians ought never to focus solely on the bottom-line consequences of their acts.

God has called us to live rightly, pleasing Him as we allow Him to conform us to Christ. Salvation full and free moves beyond forgiveness of sins. Christ's redemption grants us "the possibility of realizing the entire truth of our being," the freedom from sin's bondage for which we are fundamentally designed.[14]

In the covenant's fulfillment there is freedom. Redeemed through the grace of God, we are set free to live in accord with the plan of our Master, Christ Jesus, our Lord.

Background Scripture:
Exodus 3:1-14; 19:5-
6; 24:4-8; Acts 17:28

*Old
Covenant*

CHAPTER 2

THE COVENANT CONTEXT: GOD IS PRESENT

BY NATURE WE ARE SOCIAL BEINGS. Designed to live in community, we shun isolation, sensing the ultimate anguish of solitary confinement. From the moment of our birth we struggle with the anxiety that comes from separation, from the aloneness that marks a new creature. In truth, we live and die individually; we can never fully escape the shell of our uniqueness. So there is an inescapable, aching aloneness, like the emptiness of a deep cavern, carved into the heart of the human condition. Like death, it opens for us a window on reality, the ultimate issues of life, for at the Judgment we'll each be judged as a particular person, not as a digit in a crowd.

Still, it's painful to be alone! In the deepest level of our souls, when they ache, there is an empty space. Throughout life, for a variety of reasons we feel lonely. Only the lonely—and that's most of us at times—know the pains of separation, isolation, the feeling of being unknown and unwanted. Most deeply, there's a void felt by all who are estranged from God.

What's the Matter? A Matter of Facelessness!

Loneliness, of course, has little to do with being alone. Solitude uniquely restores and refreshes us. We often need time alone, time to be by ourselves, to be ourselves; we need interludes of reflection and contemplation. Amazingly, we are loneliest in a crowd. That's because we hunger for more than crowds of faceless folks, even when they applaud us. We hunger for a face that assures us we're real and have worth.

Living in San Diego, I sometimes see televised reports of sailors returning home after months at sea. The camera first shows hundreds of them peering intently toward the shore. Next it shows hundreds of women and children peering toward the ship. Then, at magical moments, the faces light up. Men see their wives; wives spot their husbands. With recognition comes transformation, for faces that strained to see suddenly fill with life when they see their beloved.

What Matters: Faces

Loneliness, isolation end when we see a face we know, a face that knows us. Faces, you see, are peculiar. Just study the peculiarity of the face of the next person you meet. Some of you perhaps feel offended, for sometimes we think "peculiar" means strange or odd, but that's not the root meaning of the word. "Peculiar" means distinctive and unique, belonging to one person. It's one of the majesties of creation that every face is unique, that every face is peculiarly one person's.

Consider, for example, how differently we see elbows. I've seen lots of elbows in my life, but not one of them has proved memorable. I doubt that I'd be able to pick out my wife's elbows in a lineup of them! One elbow is pretty much like any other one to me.

But faces are memorable. Most of us remember (or at least claim we remember) faces better than names. That's because faces are peculiar, unique, and distinctive, more so than names. The first thing most of us notice when we see another person is his or her face, for faces are revealing.

Our faces reveal our ancestry. Yet there's a sense in which we also shape our faces. Each of us helps carve the wrinkles and crinkles, form the muscles and flesh, the body that bears witness to our being. Our experiences, our choices leave traces on our faces. The wisdom of age lines the creases and wrinkles of saintly faces. A senior citizen's facial lines often reveal either dissipation or discipline, wasteful diversions or wise devotions. (One lady, however, asked an understandable question: "If God had to give a woman wrinkles, why couldn't He put them on her feet instead of on her face?")

Most important, faces reveal presence. The strangers I meet on sidewalks, strangers whose eyes rarely meet mine, aren't really present to me. When someone I know turns his or her back on me, hides his or her face from me, that person withholds his or her presence. But when I recognize a person and that person recognizes me, there's presence. That's what we long for—the presence of a person who affirms our being, the presence of a person who stands out from his or her surroundings, the presence of a person who confirms our standing, the reality of our being and worth.

The Glory of His Presence

One of the great revelations of Scripture about the Judeo-Christian faith is this: *God is present.* He's here. He presents himself as a gift to us. That truth permeates the Book of Exodus. The central message of the book declares that God is always and everywhere *with* His people. That message leaps from the pages of chapter 3, where we find Moses herding his father-in-law's sheep: "He led the flock to the far side of the desert and came to Horeb, the mountain of God. There the angel of the LORD appeared to him in flames of fire from within a bush" (vv. 1-2).

His curiosity piqued, Moses checked it out. Then the Lord spoke from within the bush, "Moses! Moses!" So Moses said, "Here I am." Then God said, "Do not come any closer. . . . Take off your sandals, for the place where you are standing is holy ground" (vv. 4-5). At this, Moses hid his face in fear. At that point God told Moses He planned to rescue the children of Israel and give them a Promised Land—and Moses was to lead them! The Lord assured him, saying, "I will be with you" (v. 12). Needing still more assurance, however, Moses wondered what to say if his people asked, "What is his name?" And "God said to Moses, 'I AM WHO I AM'" (vv. 13-14).

In this marvelous moment, what we call a theophany (God's self-disclosure), Moses sensed the manifest presence of God. The Hebrew language uses the same word for both "presence" and "face." On the slopes of Mount Horeb Moses encountered God. He's the One who is, the God with a face, the One who always has been and always will be, the One who is always and everywhere with us and for us.

In a way, the world and our experience in it resemble one of those picture puzzles I pondered as a child. There was a picture that looked like a jungle, full of trees and vines. If I studied it, I'd suddenly see the images of a lion, then a giraffe, then an elephant, then a big-game hunter—all curiously concealed within it. And that's our world: a visible sign of an invisible reality, a visible puzzle containing an elusive image. It's a world filled with the presence of the One who is.

The good news from God's Word for all of us is this: Whatever our situation, however dismal our predicament, God is present. He's right here with us.

Rightly approached, everything touches on the eternally real, the one Lord of all, whose Being sustains all beings. The One who is comes to us, as He came to Moses, in the midst of our ordinary routines, suddenly speaking from a common bush. But most of us are so absorbed in our problems and fantasies that we fail to see the burning bushes on the slopes of our lives.

In your world, in my world, God is here. For He is. He's the only One who is simply the great I Am. He's the One in whom "we live and move and have our being" (Acts 17:28). And He longs to reveal to us His manifest presence.

Christian faith is a gift from God, a divine present. It's a gift of God's here-and-now reality, His living presence. He would like to give us that gift if we would but turn aside and pause to see Him.

A Covenanting God—a Covenant People

During the late 1960s, to justify American involvement in Vietnam, United States President Lyndon Johnson declared we had a moral obligation, because of treaties we had signed, to defend South Vietnam. Treaties, he said, are like sacred vows—and America has never broken its treaty agreements.

At that point thousands of Native Americans fell out of their chairs in laughter. (My Cherokee-Sioux ancestry may be injecting some biases here!) Native Americans have good memories. They've kept track of the treaties made—and broken—by the United States. As a bumper sticker says, "Broken Treaty Score: Whites 398; Indians 0." No contest!

Much of the tragedy of Native American history, indeed all human history, lies rooted in the reality of broken treaties, broken promises, broken vows. In international relations, in human relations, in divine-human relations, one of the enduring evils is the persistence of broken promises. Sadly enough, there's an accuracy to the jaded cynicism of the French soldier-statesman Charles de Gaulle, who rightly compared treaties with roses and pretty young girls: "They last," he said, "while they last."[1]

Yet we humans have the unique ability to make promises. We do so continually. We rely on promises.

Nothing gives us more hope, more comfort, than their expected fulfillment. Conversely, nothing devastates us more completely than broken promises, broken vows. So it ought not surprise us, when we turn to Holy Scripture, to find that the God who is really present makes promises. He's a promise-making, covenanting God. And He wants to draw us into a covenant bond with himself.

The Terms: God's Ways with His World

In the 19th chapter of Exodus we find Moses and the Israelites, just liberated from slavery in Egypt, encamped in front of Mount Sinai—in the same area where Moses had earlier encountered the Lord in the burning bush. Now, leading his people, Moses needed God's guidance. On the mountain, the Lord reminded Moses of His holy acts of delivering Israel from bondage. Then He called them to "obey me fully and keep my covenant" so as to enjoy His presence and His world, wherein they would be for Him "a kingdom of priests and a holy nation" (vv. 5-6).

In this episode God extended His covenant to the children of Israel. The covenant message first announced to Noah, then to Abraham, then to Moses, is here extended to the Israelites at Mount Sinai. Such a covenant in the ancient world was a political agreement, cemented by vows of lasting fidelity. God offered the Israelites—and through them to us, their spiritual heirs—a real deal.

Many of us have difficulty with the ancient idea of covenant because we've been soured by politicians and political deals. We're pretty confident God would never resemble the politicians we know whose words rarely ring true. Most of what politicians promise we instinctively disbelieve, for it seems they spend half their time making promises and the other half making up excuses as to why they can't keep their promises.

But God's covenant, though detailed in treaty terms, offers more than political promises. God offered Israel a real deal—the reality of His presence. He promised to be with them, to lead them to the Promised Land. He promised to enable them to become what He had planned for them from the beginning—His children.

In exchange for His presence God asked His people to be faithful, to respond to Him. So He offers himself to us, as brides and grooms offer themselves to one another, through a covenant, through freely given promises. Later on in Israel's history, when the prophets spoke of covenant, they used the symbol of marriage, rather than of treaties, to illustrate God's ways with His people.

Marriage, rightly entered, is a covenant, not a contract. We're more familiar with contracts, of course. When we buy cars or take out loans or accept jobs, we sign contracts. They briefly bind us together to secure some mutually profitable objective. Rarely do we much care about the personal rapport established by a contract. Business contracts have worth, but they are inevitably for a limited purpose. So if we try to establish personal relationships through contracts, we court disaster. When people marry in a contractual fashion, they rarely stay married.

Covenants, however, unite persons differently than contracts. Covenants bind together people who want lasting, loving relationships, not personal dividends. Covenants unite persons who acknowledge their differences, their inequalities; who seek to give rather than get; who sense a sacred dimension to the vows they take, knowing they deal with permanent, eternal realities. Through Moses on Mount Sinai, the Lord entered into a covenant with His people. He made promises designed to last eternally.

Several years ago a man resigned his position as president of a seminary. He did so to devote himself full-time to caring for his wife of 42 years, then stricken with Alzheimer's disease. Though some well-intending friends urged him to place her in a health-care institution so that he might continue his important ministry, he decided his first calling was not to ministry but to marriage. He then devoted each day to caring for her, as a parent must care for a small child. He found, despite the discomfort, that "[my wife] is the joy of my life. Daily I discern new manifestations of the kind of person she is, the wife I always loved. I also see fresh manifestations of God's love—the God I long to love more fully."[2]

That's what we mean by covenant—fidelity!

The Blood Covenant-Monument

Whenever we make promises, we seem drawn—almost instinctively—to inscribe them on monuments, drawing symbols of personal vows that remind us we are participants in the reality of covenant. Later, if we break our covenants, we usually demolish the monuments earlier raised. After a divorce, former lovers often take their wedding bands and hock them, or they get a jeweler to reshape the diamonds and gold into something—anything—other than a symbol of wedlock.

Living covenants, binding promises, prompt us to build monuments to enshrine or sanctify them. When we marry, something more than convention impels us to have wedding ceremonies, for marriage means more than living together. Marriage testifies to a hunger for permanence. A wedding formalizes two persons' intention to sink the foundation of their love to bedrock, something deeper than the waves of life. Years ago a couple married atop the Rock of Gibraltar; the groom explained, "We chose the site because we wanted to found our marriage on a rock." Good decision!

We try to symbolize something in a wedding, something that transcends the routine agreements we make with friends and business associates. Ceremonies point to realities. When we make promises, we want to make them public, to sanctify them somehow by including witnesses who know the truth about our vows. We literally long to etch our promises into concrete as evidence of the permanence of our commitment.

Similarly God, in the process of extending His covenant to His people, established a monument—a visible symbol—to stand forever, a witness to it. He set up an altar, a blood-bathed monument, to His life-giving commitment to humanity.

The Monument: A Blood-Bathed Altar

Having announced the covenant in Exodus 19, God revealed to Moses its contents in chapter 20—the Ten Commandments. Then, in chapter 24, God revealed through a dramatic symbol the enduring means by which we keep the covenant.

Moses, we read, "built an altar at the foot of the mountain" (v. 4). Here they "sacrificed young bulls" (v. 5). Then Moses "took the Book of the Covenant and read it to the people," who said, "We will do everything the LORD has said; we will obey" (v. 7). Then he "took the blood, sprinkled it on the people and said, 'This is the blood of the covenant that the LORD has made with you'" (v. 8).

Altars stand at the center of Israel's life. More than 400 times in the Old Testament we find altars constructed, altars that physically represent God's covenant with His people. Unlike the mythical speculations of some religions, Israel's faith had rock-hard substance. God's promises to Noah, to Abraham, to Moses took physical form in altars. Moses made altars of earth or unhewn stones, using the earth's natural materials rather than humanly designed artworks. If we remember that Exodus proclaims the reality of God's presence, it's clear that anywhere there is earth and stone, we can build altars to commemorate His presence.

If we fail to build altars appropriate to God, we turn to building altars to sun and moon or various facets of ourselves. We worship what we esteem or admire. Whatever we consider most worthy becomes the object of our religion, for religion is the means whereby we try to retie the inner bond with reality that we sense has been broken. Human nature requires religion as much as it needs nutrition. We may choose to eat junk food or healthy food, but we will eat! Just as we can eat right things or wrong things, so, too, we can worship the right One or wrong things.

Our society abounds with misguided worshipers, men and women giving worth and life service to less than ultimate ends. Years ago I asked a class of students to list the things they most wanted to learn in life. Many responded by saying they most wanted to know how to live happily, how to love rightly, how to enjoy God forever. One student, that year's star basketball player, took another tack. He wanted, he said, to know how to shoot a basketball better, to pass a basketball better, to dribble a basketball better, to maneuver a basketball down the court and into the hoop somehow. Nothing else in life concerned him. In his world, success rolled with a ball to a hoop. Success has always been an object of worship.

To worship, we build appropriate places. Many modern buildings—banks, office complexes, sports arenas—address deeply religious desires. Throngs of concertgoers often seek some sort of spiritual comfort. Years ago on television I saw a man interviewed who was deeply distressed that he had not received the seats he sought at a Neil Diamond concert. This man had stood in line for hours to buy the tickets he thought would get him close to the stage. When asked why it was so important to be close to Neil Diamond, he said, "My brother died last summer, and I just had to hear Neil sing 'He Ain't Heavy—He's My Brother.'"

This man may never go to church, but he needs to find some way to cope with death, so he goes to a concert! It's a place of worship, a place with an altar. Such shrines say much about us. Tragically, future generations may be appalled at our tawdry shrines, our tinsel altars.

Covenant Altars, Where Blood Is Shed

Our secular altars lack power because they lack life. They celebrate tinsel-toned illusions. They promote distractions. They evade life's deepest realities. But the altars erected in the Bible had blood on them. That's why they were built. They absorbed the blood that was splashed on them.

Because we understand blood's life-giving power, we understand its spiritual symbolism. When we want to express lasting friendship, we call someone a blood brother. There is power in blood, and there is power in the symbols associated with blood. In the Old Testament covenant, the blood poured on the altar signified God's extended, enduring forgiveness. The blood sprinkled on the people represented their willingness to obey the Lord, to uphold the covenant.

We humans need forgiveness. We also long for something, or Someone, to give ourselves to. We want to surrender, to obey, not out of fear, but to claim the promises. We can deal with the past only with forgiveness, and we can face the future only with hopes rooted in promise. To deal with the past, we must forgive; to face the future, we must be capable of making and keeping promises. Forgiveness frees us for life.

There's a story of a man who threw a rock at a stray dog to chase it away. He threw more accurately, more forcefully, than he had intended and hit the dog, breaking its leg. Instead of running away, however, the dog limped back and licked his hand. "That day," he said, "I truly understood the meaning of God's unfailing love." In truth, the Bible declares, God is merciful. He forgives! And that eternal truth took form in a monument, in a testament, on altars, where the innocent blood of animals was spilled to atone for human sins.

Background Scripture:
Psalms 27:4; 90:1-2;
103:1; Mark 12:28-30;
Romans 8:38-39; He-
brews 8:13; 2 John 6

Old Covenant

New Covenant

CHAPTER 3

THE PROMISE PERFECTED: A NEW COVENANT

THE DISCOMFORT OF AGING results not from the fact that time passes quickly but that it lumbers its way so slowly through pointless routines. We do the same old things over and over again. We get up. We go to work. We come home and go to bed. We've done it mechanically, measuring out our lives, as T. S. Eliot said, with coffee spoons. Yet the routines grow progressively more meaningless. We who are not old fear old age, I suspect, not only because the end of life draws near but also because we fear we'll have to admit we've never truly lived.

When empty routines drive our days, time's a drag, life's a bore. If we're paralyzed by the past, if we're passé about the future, each day brings us little more than toast and tea—and we measure out our lives with coffee spoons.[1] Yet we really don't want that. We don't want to be bystanders, growing old with nothing to show for it but wrinkled coats and yellowed retirement checks. In fact, few of us want to grow old. Since we love life, we fear the loss of life that old age implies.

Some good things, we know, need refurbishing, reviving. They age, they become old, but they are too valuable to discard. They need to be overhauled and made new. If I break my arm, for instance, I don't need an arm transplant—I need the fracture fixed. The reset bone, wonder of wonders, will mend so as to make the broken spot stronger than ever. Life, however much we enjoy it, relentlessly runs down. Its brokenness needs mending. We need a transcendent remaking, a recovery of our true life—our image-of-God life.

The New Covenant

It's in this sense that we Christians understand the old covenant as expressed in the Hebrew Scriptures. We are indeed people of a new covenant; but the old covenant, one of the central components of Israel's faith, remains embedded in the new. The very division of the Bible—Old and New Testaments—reveals that fusion, for we root our faith in both the Hebrew and Christian Scriptures. We do so because we believe that the New Testament is like a seed in the pod of the Old Testament and the Old Testament flowers forth in the New.

This theme helps shape the Book of Hebrews, the Christian text that deals most thoroughly with the new covenant. Outlining how Jesus perfectly fulfills the Old Testament law, Hebrews portrays Jesus as the perfect High Priest, doing once and forever what no purely human priest had been able to do, conclusively establishing the new covenant. The old covenant needed something more—an overhaul. The broken bone needed resetting. As we read in Hebrews 8, the new covenant promises full forgiveness, making "obsolete" (v. 13) the old.

The Old Covenant (as Promised) Perfected

The old covenant was largely external and performance based. There were commandments, formal obligations that sustained the God-Israel bond. Yet doing things just because we're told to do them always leaves something lacking in a relationship.

The people of God had a relationship with Him under the old covenant. Still they frequently failed to uphold their half of the agreement; they failed to obey His law. So something new was needed. The old needed renewing, and that meant the law needed to become an inner principle—freely followed, fully embraced, and as active as yeast in the heart and mind.

Still more: the new covenant provided the intimacy between God and humans so necessary for vital spirituality. Under the old covenant, people learned about God through teachers. Under the new covenant, we can actually know God intimately. We can enter into, become one with, know God through personal communion.

And that's exactly what God seeks to establish in the new covenant, effected by Jesus Christ for us. This new life, this new covenant, comes to us through God's gracious forgiveness. Partially available under the old covenant through yearly rituals, full forgiveness forms the basis of the new covenant. Solely because He loves us, God in Christ has forgiven us. It's the new covenant, established not by the animal sacrifices of the old covenant but by the internalized intimacy and freeing forgiveness brought to us by the new covenant.

To Perfect the Promise: Give God Agapē!

Many of us at times feel we're born losers. But we're not! We may choose to lose, but we're not born to lose. We are, however, born *lovers.* So the question is not "Will we love?" but "What, how, and how well will we love?" The right ordering of love stands at the center of covenant theology, for our response to the God of love, who invites us into covenant, is the response of love.

The Greek language is a finely nuanced, precise language. Whereas English has only one word "love," whose meaning must be determined by its context, the Greeks (and thus the writers of the New Testament) used several words to clearly indicate their intent. In the Bible the word *agapē,* meaning godly love, signifies the highest form of love. It's a benevolent, unselfish commitment to another's well-being. It's the basic reality of the universe, and it's the principal ingredient of scriptural holiness. In essence, holiness is the singular will to love God above all else.

When Jesus said the greatest commandment is to love God, He used the word *agapē.* In Mark 12 a scribe asked Him, "Of all the commandments, which is the most important?" (v. 28). Jesus said, "The most important one . . . is this: 'Hear, O Israel, the Lord our God, the Lord is one. Love the Lord your God with all your heart and with all your soul and with all your mind and with all your strength'" (vv. 29-30).

To formulate our understanding of agapē, let's use the letters of the word to start other words that indicate how it brings together and perfects all that's good in love. Agapē is, I think, **a**ttentive, **g**rateful, **a**vailable, **p**ersuaded, and **e**ternal.

Agapē is attentive. To love God, we must give Him more than a passing glance. Love turns to face its beloved. "One thing I ask of the LORD," David said, "this is what I seek: that I may dwell in the house of the LORD all the days of my life, to gaze upon the beauty of the LORD and to seek him in his temple" (Psalm 27:4). Agapē attends to God, notices Him, gives Him a lingering look.

Rightly attentive, love is aware of whatever or whoever it loves. Attention is one of love's ligaments, running like a strong strand of muscle through it; and attention directed to God wraps itself in the form of prayer. Prayer is being attentive to God. We love God by giving Him our attention, our "prayer-full" attention. If you *agapaō* (the verb form of agapē) God, you give Him more than a glance; you give Him your attention. You pray.

Agapē is grateful. Lovers spontaneously praise their loved ones. They are delighted with them just for being what they are. So David declared, "Praise the LORD, O my soul; all my inmost being, praise his holy name" (Psalm 103:1).

Grateful lovers acknowledge their debts, admit their dependencies, give thanks for others' goodness. Often we fail to notice things until they are gone, fail to notice others' kindnesses until they are gone. A woman got onto a crowded bus. Obviously exhausted, she reached up to take hold of the overhead bar, since all the seats were taken, when a man offered her his seat. Totally shocked at such chivalry, the woman fainted. After she revived and took the offered seat, she thanked the man—at which point he fainted! Gratitude, it seems, does not flood the world. We're so tempted to think we're making it on our own that we fail to notice how often others help us. Sometimes it takes a shock of some sort to jolt us into gratitude.

But agapē needs no jolts. Agapē takes notice and gives thanks. Agapē praises God, the God from whom all blessings flow. Agapē simply praises as it goes.

Agapē is available. Lovers somehow find time for one another. Lovers eagerly wait upon, wait for, do things with, and do things for the one they love. We're literally at the disposal of the ones we love. So John said, "This is love: that we walk in obedience to his commands" (2 John 6).

A state forester, checking boundary lines in an isolated area of northern California, walked up a dirt road to find the landowner of a homestead adjoining state property. At the gate he found signs: "Private Property—No Trespassing!" Along the path other signs declared, "Keep Out—This Means You!" and "Beware of Dog!" Having a job to do, the forester pressed on to the cabin, where he met and talked with the property owner, who turned out to be unusually talkative and friendly. His mission accomplished, the forester prepared to leave, and the landowner kept talking. Finally, needing to get on with his work, the forester reached the door, and the landowner said, "Come and see me again sometime. I don't get many visitors up this way."[2]

Many of us have Private Property—No Trespassing! signs nailed on the gateposts of our lives. Keep Out—This Means You! rather leaps from our countenances. Some of us even have Beware of God signs! But love takes down such signs. Love makes me available to my beloved, moves me to offer him or her my life, molds me in service to the one I love.

Agapē is persuaded. Love carries its own assurance, knows some things for sure. Thus Paul declared, "I am convinced that neither death nor life . . . nor anything else in all creation, will be able to separate us from the love of God that is in Christ Jesus our Lord" (Romans 8:38-39).

There's a certainty to love. Lots of things about God I don't really understand. At times I wish He would dramatically reveal himself to me. Yet though many things are unknown, faith in God is not accepting some scientific or philosophical idea. It's falling in love with Jesus. And we can know we're in love. We can know when we are loved. There is a certainty to it all. Love is persuaded.

There is also a confidence in love. It's amazing how hopeful we become when we fall in love. Love breeds confidence. Love nurtures hope. Someone has said that people tend to see life as either a problem or a privilege. Well, lovers rejoice in life's privileges. They walk confidently into an unknown future because they walk hand in hand with someone they trust. So agapē is persuaded.

Agapē is eternal. The ad that declares, "Diamonds are forever," exaggerates, though diamonds will last longer than a new car, the current best-selling novel, or the latest rock-and-roll star. We're drawn to diamonds, I suspect, as a symbol for love because we have a deep longing for forever, for a love that lasts forever. Thus the psalmist says, "Lord, you have been our dwelling place throughout all generations. Before the mountains were born or you brought forth the earth and the world, from everlasting to everlasting you are God" (90:1-2). In our hearts we know that love, when it's real, is forever.

In the summer of 1980 a young lady was stabbed seven times and strangled to death in her Miami apartment. She was 38, had a good job, and lived the "swinging single" life. In the words of a bumper sticker, she was a "party animal." She seemed to live the "good life" portrayed in television soaps and ads. But in death she left a diary that disclosed that under the facade of a party animal was a lonely person. She had 59 lovers in the final 56 months of her life.

Yet she confessed in her diary, "I would like to have . . . once before I pass through my life the kind of a sexual relationship that is part of a loving relationship." Still more: "I'm alone," she wrote, "and I want to share something with somebody."[3] This young lady longed for a love that lasts. We all long for a love that lasts eternally; we long for God. We want Agapē, Love itself.

What does God want from us? How do we respond to His offered covenant? That's simple! Give Me agapē, says He! Such love comes from the God who is love. We can love God, we can give Him agapē, when we allow Him—Agapē itself—to fill us.

The one thing that makes us holy, the one thing that counts for eternity, the one thing God desires of men and women, is agapē. Such love comes into focus when we reflect on the Ten Commandments, the 10 Words given to Moses on Mount Sinai shortly after the deliverance of the Israelites from Egyptian bondage. Their newly discovered freedom, their newly discerned opportunity to enter into a covenant relationship with God gained substance and direction from the commandments inscribed on a stone tablet. So having stressed the importance of covenant, the context for the commandments, we now turn to a study of the Ten Commandments, considering both their Old Testament and New Testament implications, in an effort to understand how then we should live.

Key Scripture: Exodus 20:3

Background Scripture:
Joshua 24:14-15, 24; Luke
9:57-62

You shall have no other gods before me.

CHAPTER 4

A SACRED TRUST

OLD TESTAMENT FOUNDATION: NO OTHER GODS

In 1980 Bob Dylan received a Grammy Award for Best Male Rock Vocal Performance. The evening's climax, in many observers' minds, came when Dylan, greeted by a standing ovation, strode to the stage and sang "Gonna Have to Serve Somebody."

Dylan's right. You're gonna have to serve somebody! I'm gonna have to serve somebody. We choose whom or what we serve—but we can't choose not to serve.

Life is ultimately a matter of worship. We live according to what we think matters. We worship what we ultimately esteem or admire. That to which we attribute worth we worship. Martin Luther declared that whatever our hearts embrace and trust becomes our God.

In religious expressions we seek, in often complex and bizarre ways, to retie the bond with reality that we sense has been severed. The root of the Latin word *religare* means "to tie back," so when we feel "at loose ends," we try to reconnect things. We're simply born with a longing for ultimate reality that religion seeks to fulfill.

As human beings, we're both spiritual and physiological. We may eat sugar cookies or whole wheat bread, but we will eat something. We may choose to breathe carbon monoxide in a closed garage or pure air in the mountains, but we will breathe something. We may serve the devil, or we may serve the Lord, but we will serve somebody. We will worship something, but only One, the Bible says, really deserves our worship—God.

God, Our Center/Creator

This truth stands out in the last chapter of Joshua, which describes conditions in Canaan after the Israelites had conquered the Promised Land. Just before Joshua died, he renewed the covenant at Shechem. After recounting their history, he declared, "Now fear the LORD and serve him with all faithfulness. Throw away the gods your forefathers worshiped beyond the River and in Egypt, and serve the LORD. But if serving the LORD seems undesirable to you, then choose for yourselves this day whom you will serve. . . . But as for me and my household, we will serve the LORD" (24:14-15).

To this the people responded, "We will serve the LORD our God and obey him" (v. 24). Thus they reaffirmed the first of the Ten Commandments: "You shall have no other gods before me" (Exodus 20:3). The first word of liberation through law is to discover the freedom of truth about God.

Just as a circle can have only one center, so, too, the universe has only one Creator, the sole Source of all that is. By worshiping one God, we necessarily refuse to worship "other gods."

Rival Gods Rejected

Though much has changed since Israel entered Canaan 3,200 years ago, the "other gods" have stayed much the same. Whenever we humans worship "other gods," they are generally of two sorts: intellectual or sensual. They satisfy either our mind's curiosity or our body's lust, our desire to know or our desire to control. So we deify ideas or instincts; we revere either human energies or natural physical forces.

Intellectual Gods—Baal's Heirs

We're intelligent creatures, and we forever hunger to know where we come from, why we're here. The ancient world's gods were designed to meet folks' desire to know the ultimate source of life. In ancient Egypt the sun god, Amon-Re, was considered the creative power shaping and sustaining all that is. In Canaan people worshiped Baal, conceived as the mysterious life force taking form in ripening wheat, grapes, olives. They understood that life comes to us from a mysterious source, an impersonal force, and they worshiped their idea, their explanation of nature.

Today few folks consciously worship statues such as Amon-Re and Baal. They just resurrect, rename, and worship the same ideas. Whenever we believe that a purposeless, natural force created the world, we in fact worship old Amon-Re or Baal. For over a century philosophical Darwinism has challenged the theological creationism espoused by traditional Christianity. Many in the scientific community have, generally speaking, embraced Darwin's general notion of species randomly evolving through natural selection.

Darwinists insist "God had nothing to do with evolution."[1] As they at times confess, "Evolution is, in short, the god we must worship."[2] To such worshipers the Bible declares, "You shall have no other gods before me."

Sensual Gods—Erotic Baals

In addition to intellectual gods, we easily worship gods who satisfy our lusts, especially our desire to control things. In ancient Egypt there was Isis, the fertility goddess. In ancient Canaan there were many baals, subordinate to the high god Baal, who were usually worshiped through fertility rituals and sexual frenzies. Temple prostitutes and religious orgies pervaded the paganism of antiquity.

Certainly the ancient deification of the sex goddess has revived and gained advocates in modern societies. Sigmund Freud reduced the mystery of personality to sexuality, and his more radical disciples urged followers to find life's meaning by casting aside inhibitions and discovering the "joy of sex." We even have "temples"—striptease joints, dotting the alleys and access roads of urban North America, apparently attracting droves of devotees on a daily basis.

Since our sexual desire is enormously powerful, we all too often rationalize our sexual behavior rather than restrain it to live right. Though sexual sin in itself does great harm, the "most insidious corruption" weakening our species is "the corruption of the mind" that accompanies the rationalizing process. "One moves all too easily from sexual sins, which are probably the most common to [humanity], to intellectual sins, which are the most pernicious."[3] We construct idols that sanctify our desires.

Psychoanalysis, founded by Sigmund Freud and Carl Jung, stamps modernity like a trademark. One author claims that Jung's 40-year adulterous relationship with a woman and Freud's allegedly incestuous affair clearly helped shape their sexually permissive, rationalizing psychologies. Carefully examined, some of Freud's most significant theories have absolutely no basis in historical or anthropological fact. Actually, "The oldest and ethnologically most primitive people . . . tend to be monotheistic and monogamous, and even refer to God as 'Our Father.'"[4]

When we consider the gods of antiquity, comparing them with those of modernity, it's clear some things persist throughout human history. There's something latent within human nature that leads us to look for gods who validate our desires. We deify ideas or instincts. We construct sophisticated ideas to explain natural processes, or we elevate elemental instincts, especially our sexual desires.

In truth, we're "gonna have to serve somebody." Or as

Joshua said, "Choose for yourselves this day whom you will serve."

NEW TESTAMENT INTERNALIZATION: SERVE GOD

Turning to the New Testament, we see that the first commandment gains a Christian imperative in the call to discipleship. In responding to the call of Jesus, we find a singular commitment to service, an exclusive allegiance to Him, which makes more personal and intimate the command to put God first in our lives. In the Christian life, as in other realms of reality, priorities establish the quality of existence.

John Wooden of the University of California, Los Angeles (UCLA), perhaps the greatest ever to coach college basketball insists that as a coach he rarely talked about winning. What he stressed was giving one's all. And if you can get five well-coached, physically talented basketball players to give their all, you do in fact win a lot of games. The secret to success is commitment to excellence.[5]

What's true on the basketball court is also true in the physics lab. "The laws of physics should be simple," said Albert Einstein in a lecture.

"But what if they are not simple?" someone asked.

Said Einstein, "Then I would not be interested in them."[6] Einstein wanted to comprehend the cosmos, to read the mind of God, so he couldn't clutter his mind with trivial data.

To play basketball well, to do physics well, to live well, to love well—whatever we do well demands singular commitment. It demands our all. It's all or nothing at all! Still more: to follow Jesus calls for nothing less than our all. When C. S. Lewis found himself captivated by God, he also sensed that "total surrender, the absolute leap in the dark, were demanded. The reality with which no treaty can be made was upon me. The demand was not even 'All or nothing.' . . . Now, the demand was simply 'All.'"[7]

So Jesus' words in Luke 9:57-62 illuminate the "allness" of the great commandment, which is that we are to love the

Lord our God with all our heart, soul, mind, and strength. In the New Testament the old covenant, including the Ten Commandments, is fulfilled as the law of the Lord is internalized and amplified in the lives of Jesus' followers. For if we love God rightly, we'll have no problems with "other gods."

Tune Out! Toss Off the Tyranny of Pleasure

Luke's Gospel says, "As they were walking along the road, a man said to him, 'I will follow you wherever you go.' Jesus replied, 'Foxes have holes and birds of the air have nests, but the Son of Man has no place to lay his head'" (9:57-58).

This wanna-be disciple feared discomfort. Human beings, in general, allow the pleasure principle to reign like a dictator over them. The prospective disciple illustrates this. He rather liked what he saw in Jesus, thinking it might be nice to tag along. But Jesus sensed the man's commitment to comfort. We, like him, too regularly choose comfort, ignoring its hidden costs. If it feels good, we do it.

There's a story about a little guy, aged seven, who informed his mother at breakfast that he had decided to drop out of school. She asked why, and he said, "Because it's too hard, it's too long, and it's too boring." In response, his mom looked long and hard into his eyes and said, "Johnny, you've just described life! Get your coat on, get out the door, and get on that bus!"

It's easy to do the easy thing. It's easier to sleep in rather than go to class, church, or work. It's easier to eat another dip of ice cream than another helping of broccoli. It's easier to drive a car than to walk a block. We're comfort addicts! But Jesus calls us to the straight and narrow way that leads to life everlasting. If we want to be His disciples, we need to find "the road less traveled," the oft uncomfortable way of the Son of God, who had "no place to lay his head.".

Turn In! Now Is Our Hour! Stop Procrastinating!

Returning to our biblical story, Jesus "said to another

man, 'Follow me.' But the man replied, 'Lord, first let me go and bury my father.' Jesus said to him, 'Let the dead bury their own dead, but you go and proclaim the kingdom of God'" (Luke 9:59-60).

The second wanna-be disciple talked things over with Jesus and wanted to go home and bury his father. In the Semitic world this expression meant the son wanted to stay at home until his father died—which could be another 40 years! Jesus' response had nothing to do with attending a scheduled funeral. The inquirer apparently wanted to live securely under his father's protection, gaining the security that would come through inheriting his father's property, and then think about following Jesus. He represents the attitude of day-by-day delay.

Too often we fritter away our lives. Day by day we expend our energies building sand castles, buying plastic jewelry that quickly collects in cardboard boxes. We flush our lives down the tube—the television tube. Television, something we should control, too often controls us. We become couch potatoes.

Comedian Fred Allen supposedly said, "Television is a device that permits people who haven't anything to do to watch people who can't do anything." Still more, he suspected that the reason TV is called a medium is that rarely is anything on it well-done![8]

I think the great threat of TV is not its evil content—though there's room for concern there. The great threat of TV is its mesmerizing ability to detach us from reality, to fixate us in fantasies, so that we literally waste away our lives. To us—to all of us immersed in videoland—Jesus says urgently, "Don't waste your life!" For now is our hour.

We're called to live in our day, to avoid putting off until tomorrow what we can do today. The world's not standing still. Nor can we! When we come to the end of our days, I wonder how we'll evaluate the time we spent watching TV, the hours invested in attending spectator sports events and concerts. Do we want to be remembered as people who wanted to be entertained?

Take Off! Cast Off the Paralysis of the Past

The third wanna-be disciple said to Jesus, "I will follow you, Lord; but first let me go back and say good-by to my family." To this Jesus replied, "No one who puts his hand to the plow and looks back is fit for service in the kingdom of God" (Luke 9:61-62).

The man in this story wanted to keep his bases covered, his options open, his security blanket in place. He wanted to go home, to keep personal ties alive, to preserve a network of personal contacts. He wanted to follow Jesus—but he also wanted to make sure his significant others weren't alienated. He feared to break with his past, to distance himself from his comfortable kinsfolk. He allowed the past to dictate the present. Like him, we are often tempted to allow old relationships and ingrained habits to dictate our future.

Rather than wasting our lives being entertained to death, Jesus calls us to new ventures. We need to live in the only time allotted us to live—in the now.

The legendary Satchel Paige, one of the greatest pitchers in baseball history, stayed athletically active until he was (some think) nearly 60 years old. Asked the secret of his longevity, he said, "Don't look back. Something may be gaining on you."[9] Life's ahead of us, not behind us. Satchel Paige suffered race discrimination and knew the indignity of not having his true talents rightly rewarded. But throughout his life he refused to grow bitter. He did what he could with what he had. And he lived by his motto.

So, too, in following Jesus there are wanna-bes and "gonna-bes." If we're to be His disciples, we must do more than "wanna be." If we do in fact follow Him, we fulfill, as New Testament believers, the first commandment: "You shall have no other gods before me" (Exodus 20:3).

Key Scripture: Exodus 20:4-5

Background Scripture: Numbers 21:8; 2 Kings 18:4; Matthew 6:19-24; Acts 20:35

> *You shall not make for yourself an idol.*

CHAPTER 5

A SACROSANCT FOCUS

OLD TESTAMENT FOUNDATION: NO IDOLS ALLOWED

On her way to the hospital to give birth to another baby, a mom told her little boy she would return with a "gift from God." A couple of days later, peering into the baby crib, the little guy seriously interrogated the new baby, saying, "Quick, little brother, before you forget—what's God like?"

Lots of us would like to know! If we could describe God, what would He look like? What image of God washes around in our heads? How do we understand Him and His ways? Are we trying to understand God perfectly, perhaps to reduce Him to something we can handle, something as predictable as the geometric deductions we mastered in high school?

We can't easily abide the ambiguity wrapped up in the ultimate mystery of God. To suggest the true infinity of God, many theologians suggest imagining God as a circle whose center is everywhere—and whose circumference is nowhere. Unfortunately, many of us tend to make ourselves God's center and our concerns His circumference!

Rather than trying to be like God, we make God like us—something much easier to accomplish. Worse yet, some of us try to reduce God to nice, manageable forms, like cookie cutters—useful idols designed to make life more comfortable. Indeed, as Martin Luther said in *Table Talk*, "We easily fall into idolatry, for we are inclined thereunto by nature, and coming to us by inheritance, it seems pleasant."[1]

Substituting Means for Ends

The second of the Ten Commandments forbids idolatry. The first commandment isolates the Object of our worship, the Source of our theology, insisting we have no other gods. The second commandment highlights the means of our worship, our liturgy. Scripture tells us that to sustain a covenant relationship with God, to live really with Him, we're not to manufacture idols imaging earthly things. "You shall not bow down to them or worship them; for I, the LORD your God, am a jealous God" (Exodus 20:5).

Religiously, we often elevate means above ends. We want to worship God, but we become obsessed with certain ways to do so—or not to do so. We devise sophisticated strategies, often of great artistic ingenuity, whereby to approach and serve God. Idolatry, rightly understood, simply means focusing on the means (how we worship) rather than the End (the One we worship).

My wife, Roberta, is a fine cook. However, since moving to San Diego, where we get "two for the price of one" coupons for meals in many restaurants, she has radically reduced her time in the kitchen. I guess she's kind of a "kitchen dropout." One of her friends gave her a slogan attached to a magnet, to be placed on the refrigerator, declaring, "Kitchen closed. Gone shopping." But when she does cook, Roberta is a fine cook.

Just imagine, however, that she decided to demonstrate her love for me by giving herself full-time to cooking. Day after day, all day long, she'd shop for the finest foods in the most exclusive specialty shops. She'd prepare unique and tasty breakfasts and dinners. Her skills as a gourmet cook would shine like a star.

In fact, she'd make sure her talents were evident to all. She'd invite numerous guests to join us at every meal—making sure they knew she was giving herself completely to cooking meals for me, showing her love for me. Further, imagine that as time went on, she became so busy preparing and serving the food, entertaining the guests, demonstrating her devotion, that she never sat down and ate with me. In fact, morning, noon, and night, she would say little or nothing to me.

Should that happen, it would be obvious that my wife had become obsessed with means—the cooking that demonstrates her good character—rather than with ends—maintaining a warm relationship with me, her husband for whom she was cooking. In truth, the really important thing about mealtime is the fact that it enables us to be together. If my wife reduced our relationship to her activity, cooking, I'd soon tire of the good food and start skipping meals, knowing she'd keep on cooking and entertaining folks because she wanted to impress the world with her devotion to me.

Similarly, we break fellowship with God when we get so obsessed with the ways we do things that we forget *why* we're doing them and for *whom* we're doing them. When we reduce God to human scale, focusing on our ways of doing things, we become idolatrous.

Years ago a now-famous singer was asked to sing in her home church in Tennessee. She was 15 years old and wanted to accompany herself with a guitar. She asked her father if she could, and he told her to ask one of the congregation's elders, for her church had traditionally allowed no musical instruments in its services. Amazingly, the elder said yes. So she sang, guitar resounding. As a result, some of the older people quit the church. The man who permitted her to sing, however, said he did so because the "no-instrument doctrine" had become an idol that needed to be broken. He thought she was the one to break it.

If we can't worship without organ music, we've made the organ an idol. If we can't worship without guitar music, we have a guitar-shaped idol. If we can't worship except to the tune of traditional hymns, we've cast them as gold-gilded idols. If we can't worship except while singing contemporary praise choruses, we've created new idols. If we refuse to listen to preachers unless they sound like certain well-known speakers, we've turned little humans into little idols.

Substituting Things for a Person

We also make idols when we revere things rather than their Creator, when we prefer gifts to the Giver, when we use persons so as to enjoy things rather than use things so as to enjoy persons.

Imagine another scenario: Imagine that years ago I had started bringing home a present for my wife each time I returned from a trip. Since I travel quite a bit, the gifts would begin to add up. Imagine that my wife expected me to bring her a gift every time I came home—and that it was evident that she wanted a nicer gift each time. If I failed to bring a present, she would not talk with me for a week. If the gift was a bit cheap, she would sulk and complain that I really didn't love her very much.

It would become clear that she spent most of her time caring for the collection of gifts: polishing them, putting them in fine display cases, talking about them with her friends, talking with me only when things were at issue. One day, as you would suspect, it would dawn on me that she cared for me only as a supplier of gifts. She really liked the stuff I bought her, not the person who brought them to her. In treasuring the things more than the person who brought them, she would fray the marriage bond, the loving commitment between two persons.

Now God created the material world, so material

things help us understand some things about Him. Many things serve as useful analogies. An anonymous person recently compiled a list of analogies, suggesting,

God is like Coca-Cola—He's the real thing.

God is like Bayer aspirin—He works wonders.

God is like Hallmark cards—He cares enough to send the very best.

God is like VO5 hair spray—He works through all kinds of weather.

God is like Dial soap—aren't you glad you know Him?

God is like Scotch tape—you can't see Him, but you know He's there.

God is like American Express—don't leave home without Him.

Such analogies are fine, even helpful, if we remember they are simply ways of imagining, as long as we remember to whom they point. In my opinion, the only way we can think at all about God is by comparison. Material things, physical symbols, artistic works effectively direct our attention to nonmaterial, nonphysical realities. Sure enough, God's the real thing! So He's sort of like Coca-Cola. But if you treat Coca-Cola as the real thing, reverently drinking the magical fluid in hopes of life everlasting, you have turned an analogy into an idol.

The Book of Numbers tells how the Israelites in the wilderness grumbled about the food (manna), wanting God to give them more palatable stuff. They complained so much that God sent poisonous snakes among them. While some folks were dying, others grew repentant and asked Moses to pray for them. In response to Moses' prayer, "The LORD said to Moses, 'Make a snake and put it up on a pole; anyone who is bitten can look at it and live'" (21:8). This Moses did, and the snake became a symbol of God's mercy. So long as it remained a symbol reminding people of God, it was a blessed memento. It was an icon, a holy symbol.

Seven centuries later, however, the snake became an idol. The people of Israel began worshiping the symbol, not the God whose mercy it represented. So King Hezekiah, when he reformed the nation, "broke into pieces the bronze snake Moses had made" (2 Kings 18:4). A marvelous sign of deliverance had been twisted into an idolatrous talisman, a thing of magic and power before which folks burned incense and worshiped.

Though we're tempted to isolate idolatry to ancient eras, in fact we live in a thoroughly idolatrous culture. Our industrial society, stamping out goods with cookie-cutter efficiency, sets before us an almost infinite number of idols that give or promise to give us infinite power. In the words of a Nicaraguan poet:

> Modern materialism is not very different from ancient polytheism, and the world has never worshipped as many idols as today. Cars, movie stars, political leaders, ideologies are the modern idols—the idols of commercial advertising and the idols of political propaganda, the smiling goddesses of fertility and material abundance, quack medicines and hygiene, the gods of beer, corn flakes and dentifrices; the faces of dictators and political bosses and the somber deities of terror and war, of destruction and death.[2]

Yet the Word of God stands: "You shall not make for yourself a graven image. . . . you shall not bow down to them or serve them" (Exodus 20:4-5, RSV). So if you're tempted to reduce God to cookie-cutter goods—useful and usable for you, the magic door to the goods of the good life—think again!

NEW TESTAMENT INTERNALIZATION: WHAT'S REALLY LIVING?

Several years ago Tony Campolo told about a man who asked to be buried seated behind the wheel of a brand-new Cadillac, dressed in a tuxedo, with a two-dollar cigar in his mouth. He left the money to insure that his wish would be fulfilled, and it was. The undertaker brought in a huge crane to maneuver the automobile-casket for the dead man. As he pulled the handle lowering the corpse and Cadillac into the ground, the crane operator was heard to say, "Man, that's really living!"[3]

I wonder what we consider "really living." To some, according to a modern T-shirt, "The one who dies with the most toys wins." In the end, we're told, what really counts is only what we can count! One historian declares that many, if not all of us, say, "What is the chief end of man? To get rich. In what way? Dishonestly if we can; honestly if we must. Who is God, the only one and true? Money is god."[4]

There is an addiction worse than alcoholism. There is a disease worse than AIDS. It's the idolatry of money, the voracious lust for money that sacrifices everything for monetary gain. In the Sermon on the Mount Jesus addressed this very issue, deepening the dimensions of the second commandment, which insisted we discard idols and worship God alone.

In Matthew's Gospel, seeking to focus our faith on God alone, Jesus calls us to the freedom of serving the Liberator-Creator rather than idols of our own creation:

> Do not store up for yourselves treasures on earth, where moth and rust destroy, and where thieves break in and steal. But store up for yourselves treasures in heaven, where moth and rust do not destroy, and where thieves do not break in and steal. For where your treasure is, there your heart will be also.

> The eye is the lamp of the body. If your eyes are good, your whole body will be full of light. But if your eyes are bad, your whole body will be full of darkness. If then the light within you is darkness, how great is that darkness!

> No one can serve two masters. Either he will hate the one and love the other, or he will be devoted to the

one and despise the other. You cannot serve both God and Money *(6:19-24).*

The word translated "money" was an Aramaic word, *mamon* (in English "mammon"), which meant material possessions. In our society it best represents a combination of "things, money, gain, or success."[5] For us, mammon means "making it."[6] At issue, of course, is not having such goods, but serving them. As Martin Luther said, "The emphasis here is on the little word 'serve.' It is no sin to have money and property, wife and children, house and home. But you must not let it be your master. You must make it serve you, and you must be its master."[7]

Jesus talked frequently about money. Sixteen of His 38 parables dealt with it; 1 out of every 10 verses in the Gospels refers to it. Though major themes, such as prayer and faith, are mentioned in 500 verses, money appears in 2,000! Clearly it was a big issue to Jesus. That's because it's so easy to serve money rather than God. Indeed, it's easy to make money our god. In our quest for happiness we're tempted to think hoarding money enables us to attain it. As another author has said, "Money is human happiness in the abstract: he, then, who is no longer capable of enjoying human happiness in the concrete devotes himself utterly to money."[8]

It's Easy to Worship/Serve Money

So we must understand that "what Jesus is revealing is that money is power."[9] The world's heroes must earn millions, for we equate success with income. They've made it, we think. We know that some of them now and then lament, "Now that I'm here, where am I?" But the rest of us still push on, assuming we'll feel differently when *we* reach the top.

In *The Day America Told the Truth,* folks responded to the question "What are you willing to do for $10 million?" Some 25 percent of the respondents would abandon their families or their churches; 23 percent would become prostitutes for a week or more; 16 percent would give up their United States citizenship; 7 percent would kill an innocent stranger.[10] Recently 3,000 women responded to an opinion poll that asked what would make their lives better. Three percent marked "a better sex life." Eight percent wanted "a different relationship." But 60 percent (more than twice the percentage of the second-place item) said, "More money." Some little girls, barely into grammar school, were asked to state their fondest wish. They could think of nothing grander than to have $5 million—and two days in a mall![11] We do, as people, love money. And we're apparently willing to serve it in various ways.

It's Essential That We Worship/Serve God Alone

Jesus, God's Son, dares us to reject the very thing our culture most admires—money. He wants us to see the realities of life. Money and success are abstractions, not realities. They're idolatrous images that we worship and pursue, but they never truly satisfy. In fact, they effectively enslave and ultimately damn us. "When we claim to use money, we make a gross error. We can, if we must, use money, but it is really money that uses us and makes us servants by bringing us under its law and subordinating us to its aims."[12]

When we fall under mammon's spell, we go astray in life. A noted economist concluded, "The pursuit of money, or any enduring association with it, is capable of inducing not only bizarre but ripely perverse behavior."[13] Consider what happened in 1930 when Henrietta Garrett died at the age of 81. She left $17 million in her estate and no will. One cousin survived, as did half a dozen friends. Yet in time 26,000 persons from 29 different countries, hiring 3,000 lawyers, tried to prove they were Mrs. Garrett's legal heirs!

In the process they perjured themselves in court, fabricated family records, legally changed their names, falsified records in church Bibles, and made up improbable tales of illegitimacy. Consequently, 12 were fined, 10 went to jail, 2 committed suicide, and 3 were murdered.[14] Idolatry exacts its price!

Rich men frequently find no joy in wealth, not because of the wealth itself, but because, as Jesus said, their eyes are darkened. Their riches, like cataracts, dim their vision. They need enlightened eyes—"good" eyes. Good eyes are "generous" (a better translation). Bad eyes are "grudging and ungenerous."[15] A good eye, a generous eye, sees money as something to use for good, not something to hoard as if it were in itself good.

When the Emperor Decius (ca. A.D. 250) was persecuting the Church, some of his emissaries barged into a church and demanded that its deacon, Laurentius, give them the treasures they had heard were buried there. In response, Laurentius pointed out the sick who were being attended, the widows and orphans getting food, and said, "These are the treasures of the Church."[16] At its best the Church and its faithful testify to the truth that "it is more blessed to give than to receive" (Acts 20:35), to have a good eye, to look for opportunities to share God's gifts.

Both windows and mirrors are made of glass. Mirrors are nice when you're getting ready to face the world in the morning. I much prefer shaving with a mirror to guide my razor. But I don't want to live in a house of mirrors. I want windows to open up my awareness of my world. To live in a windowless house would be intolerable to me. To live in a house with mirrors instead of windows would prove utterly oppressive. The only difference between the glass that enables me to see out, to see the world, and the mirror that reflects myself is a thin layer of silver behind the glass, which makes the mirror reflect.

That's what money does. It coats the windows of our hearts and minds with silver, keeping us from seeing as we ought to see, keeping us from living as we ought to live—open to and aware of the world of God and people around us.

Key Scripture: Exodus 20:7

Background Scripture: Matthew 5:37; 6:9-10; 12:35-37; Mark 16:18; Revelation 4:8, 10-11

> *You shall not misuse the name of the LORD your God.*

CHAPTER 6

A HALLOWED NAME ABOVE ALL NAMES

OLD TESTAMENT FOUNDATION: TAKE NOT GOD'S NAME IN VAIN

The third commandment says, "You shall not take the name of the LORD your God in vain" (Exodus 20:7, NASB). It could be translated, "You shall not misuse or abuse the name of God," or, "You shall not frivolously name God's name." To walk with God, we clearly must know and revere His name, for names really matter!

Relationships occur and endure only among people who know each other by name. Anonymous relationships exist no more than does love between strangers passing in the night. Loving bonds stay knit when people revere each other's names. And the most precious relationship available to us, made possible by the God who is really present with us, demands that we take not "the name of the LORD [your] God in vain."

Years ago I was ordained a minister. In our denomination, ordination services climax a district assembly and are notably solemn events, invested with sacred language and liturgy. My wife and I were kneeling, along with other ordinands, at the altar. The general superintendent came to me, placed his hand on my head, read some liturgical phrases, and intoned, "Gerald Reed, I ordain . . ." At that point the sacredness of the moment dissolved for my wife and me. We were instantly amused rather than blessed. The ordination, strangely enough, seemed irrelevant to me—for my name is Gerard, not Gerald!

I like my name. My name and I are integrally united. I've always liked my name and strongly resisted efforts to reduce it to nicknames such as Jerry. Telephone solicitors who call and warmly purr, "Hello, is this Gerald?" are coolly informed that "this is Gerard speaking!" Much of my life has been invested in correcting documents and introductions that label me Gerald.

Gerard is a French name that means "bright, shining spear," a rather militant label. It's akin to Gerhard in German, Gerardo in Spanish. My parents selected the name because they listened to a radio program that was popular in the early 1940s, *The Quiz Kids*. They liked a smart little guy named Gerard and named me for him. Whether or not I've lived up to my namesake, I like my name. Somehow it's important to me.

So if you want to initiate and cultivate a relationship with me, don't call me Gerald or Jerry! Names really matter. There's a mystical warmth generated when people remember names. And relationships survive by revering the sacredness of names. So the Bible tells us to be careful when we use God's name.

Perjury Proscribed

Most clearly, the third commandment refers to using God's name to sanctify a lie. When a person is called into court as a witness and swears on a Bible "to tell the truth, the whole truth, and nothing but the truth, so help me God," he or she assumes a sacred obligation. To commit perjury, to lie under oath, is the most obvious violation of the third commandment. As Philo wrote, "To invoke God to attest the truth of a lie is a most impious deed."[1]

Now I've never been called as a witness in a court trial. I doubt I ever will. But this commandment still applies to me, for I've made some very public vows, calling upon God as my witness, vows that I'm honor-bound to keep. When I was baptized at the age of 12, it was "in the name of the Father and of the Son and of the Holy Spirit." Taking the name of the Holy Trinity, I vowed to turn from sin and live for God.

Ten years later I stood before an altar, in the presence of God and a great company of witnesses, and promised to be faithful to my wife for the rest of my life. Were I to walk away from her, I'd be walking away from God as well, for in breaking my marriage vow, I'd be taking God's name in vain as well. Solemn vows, invoking God's name, demand we uphold the promises we've made.

Profanity Prohibited

More than perjury, profanity is also prohibited. When we profane something, we degrade what is good. Profane language degrades good words, reducing them to rubbish. The word "profane" comes from two Latin words: *pro,* meaning "before," and *fanum,* meaning "temple." To profane means to drag out holy things from the temple, to degrade them. Profanely using God's name reduces to filth the most lofty, sacred name in our language.

I wish I could say this commandment prohibits vulgar or dirty language, because I don't like dirty mouths any more than I like dirty faces or feet. Though I think we need to watch our language, to be as opposed to filthy speech as to body odor, that's admittedly more my own conviction than the meaning of the third commandment. For the profanity that's forbidden is the language that robs God's name of the sanctity due it. One author rightly insists that this commandment "is not just a nice-Nellyish warning against profanity. It is much more like the sort of warning you see around power plants: 'Danger—High Voltage!' For the ancient Hebrews seem to have thought of God almost literally as a live wire."[2]

Truly, some things are too sacred to be profaned, and some words have become taboo. Students at universities have been punished for making racially insensitive remarks. A distinguished professor had to quit teaching a class because he failed in his lectures to conform to some language about Native Americans. We are, in fact, concerned about words. The language we use, what we say about certain persons or groups of persons, matters.

Yet you can, without social disapproval—much less legal penalty—profanely use God's name! But Scripture speaks clearly: we're not to take God's name in vain by cursing. There is, of course, a strangely religious dimension to swearing. Folks who swear—even atheists who swear—indirectly invoke God. When they are angry, they might use God's name in vain but not the president's. Blasphemous language must have a deity to invoke.

Presumption Proscribed

In the third place, this commandment forbids using God's name as a magical formula, a kind of good-luck charm. Certain names carry with them an alluring power. Using powerful names enables one to manipulate things to one's own advantage. So, "What was prohibited [by this commandment] was the misuse of power."[3]

Following the Civil War, General Robert E. Lee lost virtually everything. He not only lost the war but also lost property, salary, position in society. He was, however, a war hero—even to many Northerners. Consequently, he was offered a lucrative position with a life insurance company—honorary president for life. The company offered him a good salary for no work. They only wanted to profit from the use of his name. Lee, however, refused the offer, explaining, "Gentlemen, I have nothing left but my name, and that is not for sale."[4]

Too often we want to trade upon God's name, invoking it like magic to achieve our ends. When we're sick, we claim healing in the name of Jesus, acting as if He's obligated to answer our prayer. When we're poor, we pray for wealth in the name of Jesus, assuming He's as frantic about our finances as we are. If we use God's name or His Son Jesus' name as if they were magical tools with which to gain our own desires, that's taking God's name in vain.

Still more, perhaps most important, this commandment condemns frivolous religious rhetoric, talking and using God's name in empty, vain, silly ways—ways that in fact discount the reality of His presence. We can, strangely enough, talk about God in such a way as to indicate we really don't think He's here. We can pray, using God's name, in ways that indicate we really don't think there's a divinity who hears and weighs our words.

And that's especially true for "God talk." We religious folks often get inoculated against the awe of our Subject, God! We become numbed to the majesty of what we proclaim. We fall into the trap of using religious language and the name of God to add some special allure to ourselves. Even worse, we easily use words to shape God into our own image or an image acceptable to us.

A few years ago I read a heartrending story, "When AIDS Invades the Pastor's Family," by Doug Herman. In 1985, after complications delivering their first child, his wife required two units of blood. Tragically, the blood was tainted with the HIV-III virus, which often precedes AIDS. Struggling with the issue, Doug claimed biblical promises for healing, telling his wife, "You've already been healed. When the infectious blood entered your body, it was seared clean by the healing touch of Jesus! 'They shall drink any deadly poison and it shall not harm them.' [See Mark 16:18.] That includes blood."

Knowing they were innocent of wrongdoing, giving themselves to pastoral ministry, the Hermans ignored doctors' advice and used no contraceptives, in time conceiving another child. That child tragically came into the world afflicted with AIDS and subsequently died. As Herman told the story, in his brokenness, he confessed his sorrow at presuming on God's power, at assuming he could somehow bend God's resources to his personal ends.[5]

NEW TESTAMENT INTERNALIZATION: HOW TO HALLOW GOD'S NAME

A century ago Mark Twain talked with a ruthless businessman who piously proclaimed, "Before I die I mean to make a pilgrimage to the Holy Land. I will climb Mount Sinai and read the Ten Commandments aloud at the top," to which Twain replied, "I have a better idea. You could stay home in Boston and keep them."[6]

Over 50 years ago a Texas congressman, Maury Maverick, coined the word "gobbledygook." He said, "Perhaps I was thinking of the old bearded turkey gobbler back in Texas who was always gobbledy gobbling and strutting with ludicrous pomposity. At the end of this gobble, there was a sort of gook." To illustrate gobbledygook, Maverick cited bureaucratic memos and political manifestos that seem designed to misguide. Against such perversions of our language, former Congressman Maverick protested, "A man's language is a very important part of his conduct. He should be held morally responsible for his words just as he is accountable for his other acts."[7]

Just as we know trees by their fruit, Jesus said, so too we know persons by their words: "The good man brings good things out of the good stored up in him, and the evil man brings evil things out of the evil stored up in him. But I tell you that men will have to give account on the day of judgment for every careless word they have spoken. For by your words you will be acquitted, and by your words you will be condemned" (Matthew 12:35-37).

Further note Jesus' words in the Sermon on the

Mount, in which He said, "Simply let your 'Yes' be 'Yes,' and your 'No,' 'No'; anything beyond this comes from the evil one" (5:37). One commentator said:

> All speech that moves beyond the clear yes or no has its source in the devil. This yes or no clarity also means that there is something devilish about all pedantic or painted speech that seeks to impress with its learning, cleverness, or even devotion. The devil is the author of both extremely abstruse and of extremely pious speech.[8]

Jesus detested phony speech, hypocrisy. He condemned the practice, so common in His day, of religious doublespeak. By manipulating their words, folks eluded responsibility for their promises or statements.

It's not too hard to find examples of hypocrisy. What's truly difficult is to correct it in ourselves. To say simply what you mean and mean what you say takes courage and discipline. When we deploy language as a smoke screen to evade responsibility for our actions or our promises, we become hypocrites. When we play verbal games to avoid truth about ourselves, we play the game of hypocrisy. And nothing more quickly separates us from God than verbal games—especially of the religious sort—pretending we are what we're not.

Names Really Matter and Ought to Be Hallowed

Names matter! The names we call one another mean something. Though this is true, some folks treat the matter frivolously. Some parents almost seem to delight in discomforting their kids by giving them strange names.

Some folks dislike their names enough to get them legally changed. An Arizona Native American asked a judge to give him a shorter name. "What's your name now?" asked the judge.

"Chief Screeching Train Whistle," the man replied.

"And to what do you wish to shorten it?" asked the judge.

Standing a bit taller, folding his arms across his chest, Chief Screeching Train Whistle solemnly said, "Toots."

If that story were true (and it's not), "Toots" needed to study his tribal history a bit more. Native Americans, especially those lacking written languages, believed that names revealed the essence of what was named.

When, as a young boxer, Cassius Clay converted to Islam and changed his name to Muhammad Ali, he made an important statement. He was saying that his name should reveal his inner essence, stand for his true identity. If you respect Muhammad Ali—or even if you just want to stay healthy—you'd be wise never to call him Cassius Clay. His name identifies his character as a Muslim.

So, too, we reveal our respect for God when we rightly use, when we "hallow," His name, His real nature, God as He is. The names we use referring to God mean something. So Jesus, teaching His disciples to pray, said to begin by saying, "Our Father . . . hallowed be your name" (Matthew 6:9).

How to Hallow a Name

We hallow God's name when we give Him our mind's attention. When God's name is mentioned, we turn attentive. Now God speaks to us through His Word—the written word of Scripture and the crafted word of creation. If we're interested in a loving relationship with the living God, we need to be attentive to His voice.

We also pray for God's will to become so central to us that He ignites our heart's affection. When I see Jesus living as He did, when I see Him dying on the Cross, my heart is warmed. His name is hallowed in the hollow of my heart. We also hallow God's name when we give Him our lips' adoration. We pray that He will reveal himself so as to elicit our praise. Whenever we see something truly awesome, we cannot keep from praising it.

If God is like Jesus, if the Bible properly portrays God, nothing short of adoration is in order. In the Book of Revelation, John reports that around the throne of God there is endless adoration. Four heavenly creatures "never stop saying: 'Holy, holy, holy is the Lord God Almighty, who was, and is, and is to come'" (4:8). Then "the twenty-four elders fall down before him who sits on the throne, and worship him who lives for ever and ever. They lay their crowns before the throne and say: 'You are worthy, our Lord and God, to receive glory and honor and power, for you created all things, and by your will they were created and have their being'" (vv. 10-11).

We love a person by hallowing, keeping central, his or her name. We really want to know the person as he or she is, to relate rightly to him or her.

Several years ago I asked my wife, Roberta, if she liked her name. She said no. Her parents had expected a boy and planned to name him Robert. Instead, a little girl arrived, so they named her Roberta. She's never particularly liked the name, in part because it sounds old-fashioned and outdated, and she's a very up-to-date, stylish woman.

Then I asked her what she wished her name was. She thought a moment, then said, "Trixie."

"Trixie!" I said. It's quite a revelation to find that your wife of 15 years secretly thinks she's a Trixie. So I said I didn't think I could handle Trixie and asked her what her second choice would be.

She thought a moment, then said, "Rob."

So from that moment onward I've called her Rob. For a few years she unsuccessfully tried to get friends and family to follow suit, but only a few could make the adjustment. Now she has relapsed and uses the name Roberta, but I still call her Rob.

So, too, with God. We call Him by names that adequately describe Him. We hallow His name by using it well, asking that He reveal himself to us as He really is so as to evoke our attention, our affection, our adoration.

Key Scripture: Exodus 20:8-11

Background Scripture:
Mark 2:27-28; Luke 4:4;
Acts 20:7; Hebrews 10:25;
12:2

> *Remember the*
> *Sabbath day*
> *by keeping it*
> *holy.*

CHAPTER 7

A SANCTIFIED COSMOS

OLD TESTAMENT FOUNDATION: LIVING SABBATICALLY

Loving bonds stay strong when nourished by good amounts of time together. Children need parents to spend time with them. That is the only way they can share their being. Husbands and wives too often lose their love for each other by losing touch, speeding along their separate ways. Life together requires time together.

What's true for human relationships certainly applies to our walk with God; so to help us focus on the quality of our experience with the Lord, it's helpful on a regular basis to ask ourselves this important question: "Are we finding any ecstasy in life's monotony?" To prepare us for such, the Scriptures call us to sabbatical living.

Some expect to find a good time in sensual pleasures. It's an old temptation, what Latin church fathers called concupiscence, the pleasures or lusts of the flesh. Such pleasures pass quickly and leave us with hangovers and heartaches, hardly making our lifetime good. We're also tempted to imagine that we'll settle into the "good life" when we finally collect enough possessions to feel secure. Such temptation the early fathers called covetousness. Yet neither pleasures nor possessions make time good, for the thing that makes time good is a quality of being—good living rather than having goods.

It's better to *be* than to *do* or to *have*. This is the abiding truth of biblical Sabbaths, for the Bible reminds us that we need to stop work, to relax, to simply be the persons God made us to be. Could we but learn to live at ease—sabbatically—we might learn to prefer *being* to *having*.

In that way we would imitate to a small degree our Heavenly Father. Here Scripture provides us a divine example to follow. We are to live just as God lives—at ease, resting, sabbatically. To live sabbatically means, primarily, awakening to an acute awareness of God in creation.

What makes time good? How can we make our time good? Lots of us neither tolerate nor manage time well. In the morning we can't wait for the day to pass. On Monday we can't wait for the weekend. At the beginning of the school term we can't wait for it to end. We'd often prefer not to be conscious of the dull routines of life—the minutes and hours and days of study and work, of traffic and tasks.

Though I don't approve of drunkenness, I think I understand why people drink. They find life boring and want to escape the dullness of time. Intoxication lifts one, if only for a few hours, out of the deadness of daily routines. So, too, do diversions of various sorts, insulators from time's reality.

The idea that time should, at least sometimes, be good is the central truth of one of the distinctive marks of Judaism—the biblical Sabbath. The Bible reminds us that we need to stop work, to take it easy, to simply be and to enjoy being the persons God desires us to be. "Remember the Sabbath day by keeping it holy. Six days you shall labor and do all your work, but the seventh day is a Sabbath to the LORD your God. On it you shall not do any work. . . . For in six days the LORD made the heavens and the earth . . . but he rested on the seventh day. Therefore the LORD blessed the Sabbath day and made it holy" (Exodus 20:8-11).

Regarding this text, a Jewish scholar wrote, "Judaism is a religion of time, aiming at the sanctification of time."[1] I would add that not only personally does God want to sanctify us, but also through us He wants to sanctify His world.

God's Example

The creation account reveals that God rested on the seventh day. He wasn't all worn out with exertion. He didn't need to rest up. He rested in order to enjoy what He had made. Having called into being creatures both good and beautiful, God determined to view, to interact with, to appreciate His work. He created and delighted in creation. He's present in His handiwork, wanting to be with and to enjoy the beauty and goodness of His world.

"Creation is God's work," wrote one author, "but the sabbath is God's present existence. His works express God's will, but the sabbath manifests his Being."[2] Today we need an acute awareness of God in creation. We need to discern His reality through the stillness of sabbatical living, hearing (as did Elijah on Mount Horeb, the mountain of God) the One who softly whispers out of the surrounding silences.

There's a profound difference between work time and worship time. The Greeks, whose language was often quite precise, distinguished between *chronos,* the ticking clock time we work by, and *kairos,* a suspended-animation, reflective time. Chronos time is necessary, inescapable. But like the tick, tick, tick of the clock, it's monotonous—one dull tone after another. Is anything duller than listening to an endlessly ticking clock?

Kairos, however, is time with a melody, at times an ecstasy, when we slip through a "wrinkle in time" and enter another dimension wherein clock time disappears. We discover when we experience both kinds of time that kairos is really good time. We need points of ecstasy to lighten up life's monotony.

Amazingly enough, time is really good when we lose consciousness of it. One sure measure of a good time is this: I never check my watch when I'm having a good time. I've heard a few sermons that lifted me above time; I didn't want them to end. And I've heard lectures that seemed as if they would never end. What I find in those times that I find good is a joyous delight, an ecstasy in the present moment that opens a "wrinkle in time" to eternity. For, as C. S. Lewis asks, "Where, except in the present, can the Eternal be met?"[3]

God's Exhortation

Not only did God rest on the seventh day, but also He commanded His people to remember the Sabbath, to make it holy. To sustain a covenant bond with God, we need to devote time to Him. We all know it's necessary to reserve time for those we love if we want to stay in love. So the fourth commandment is a prescription for keeping love alive.

Rightly read, the Old Testament calls for three different kinds of Sabbath: one day out of seven, one year out of seven, and a culminating jubilee year to consummate a 50-year cycle. For the reality is this: while work's necessary, it's not the only thing necessary. "Man does not live on bread alone," Jesus said in Luke 4:4. Work must be kept in its rightful place—integrated with, merely a part of, our being the persons we're called to be.

If I want to maintain a good marriage, I must spend time with my wife. In fact, the very best thing I can spend on my wife is my time. When I'm home enjoying my wife's presence, I'm unconcerned with the clock. In fact, when the evening ends and it's time to retire, I often wonder how the time slipped so quickly away! That's because I enjoy just being with my wife. And I enjoy being in the home she makes, for she is, among other things, a marvelous homemaker. To live with my wife means to relax and enjoy her presence in the world she has created.

What's true for my marriage is also true for my life in God. For me to know and enjoy God's presence, the main investment I must make is simply to take time for Him. Taking time to be with Him means relaxing and enjoying His world, His creation, the good earth and its plants and animals, its mountains and oceans. If I do so, perhaps I'll begin to see things from His perspective and live wisely and well. Perhaps I'll learn to live sabbatically.

To do this means we'll need to stop the compulsive busyness that characterizes our normal routines. We need to slow down! One of the great missionary statesmen of an earlier day had a motto in his office that said, "Beware of the barrenness of a busy life." How true! Too often our lives are barren because they're fixated on the furious quest to make money and get more things. We need simply to stop and be God's children, folks who enjoy picnics and walks in woods, simple activities that add nothing to our bank accounts.

Lots of folks in our society take off work at least one day a week (though their "rest" may not approximate the biblical model). But the second sabbatical commanded in Scripture—resting for an entire year—is almost nowhere practiced. In a technological society it probably can't be observed. But if we want to follow God's plan for humanity, we need to follow its call to ease off, to reduce our consumption so as to conserve creation.

God commanded His people to rest every seventh year, plus a jubilee every 50 years, to let creation take a rest as well. The land needs a rest. Plants and animals need time to flourish freely without human demands. Were this universally practiced, we would have far fewer ecological worries. Earth's soil is a marvelous organic mix of living creatures. Since farming wearies the soil, it needs periodic rest and restoration. One has said, "More than anything else the Sabbath rest symbolizes [human] awareness of living in God's creation."[4]

NEW TESTAMENT INTERNALIZATION: A NEW DAY FOR THE NEW WAY

Years ago my wife and I took one of my nephews to church with us. Because of the size of the crowds, the Sunday evening service was televised on a big screen in an overflow auditorium, where we sat. Later, when his folks came to get him, they asked what he had done. He said, "We saw a movie at church, but it wasn't very good."

I suspect lots of folks drop out of church because it's not very good. It's dull rather than delightful. Going to church becomes something "you gotta do" rather than a place you long to go in order to meet a special Someone. Since it's not what some define as a good time, many folks just ignore the fourth of the Ten Commandments and fail to find what is God's good time.

While looking at the Ten Commandments, we've moved between the Old Testament law and the New Testament's internalization of that law. The Sabbath commandment, at first glance, seems an exception to that pattern, for the New Testament says little about it. Yet if we see that the Sabbath was given to lift us into God's time, to help us find some out-of-time ecstasy amid the routines of life, the New Testament has something even better for us than the Old Testament's seventh-day observance.

When we read the New Testament, we discover that Jesus had little concern for rigid Sabbath restrictions. In fact, He routinely got in trouble for His Sabbath activities.

Mark's Gospel records one such incident in which Jesus was condemned because His disciples had picked some grain in a field. Jesus responded that David, though not a priest, had entered God's house and eaten "consecrated bread" reserved for priests because he needed to eat. Then He declared, "The Sabbath was made for man, not man for the Sabbath. So the Son of Man is Lord even of the Sabbath" (vv. 27-28).

We're Not Made for the Sabbath

Sabbath observance, for many people in Jesus' day, had degenerated into an almost endless list of prohibitions. Some contemporary church folks, if reared by conservative parents in conservative congregations, are tempted to think they lived under too many rules. But compared to the ancient Pharisees, virtually all Evangelicals are quite permissive!

Back then, learned rabbis had taken the fourth of the Ten Commandments, "Remember the Sabbath day by keeping it holy" (Exodus 20:8), and figured out 39 classes, with 39 subclasses under each class, of forbidden work—1,521 different tasks or activities. A farmer couldn't sow seeds or plow fields or harvest grain. A homemaker couldn't light a fire or put out a fire, knead dough or bake bread. No one could tie a knot or untie a knot.

As we might expect, these prohibitions led to some curious interpretations. For one thing, Sabbath spitting was forbidden. The Pharisees reasoned one ought not spit on the Sabbath because the one who did so might carelessly rub it with a sandal and create a ball of dirt—and that would be plowing on the Sabbath!

Some rabbis declared that one could feed chickens on the Sabbath. However, one must feed them vegetables or bread, not grain, because the chickens might miss a kernel and bury it while scratching around—thus sowing seed on the Sabbath. Use of a mirror was allowed during the week, but on Saturday no one could use it. One might be tempted to pluck an errant hair from eyebrow or beard and that would be harvesting on the Sabbath.

To the Pharisees, then, Jesus' disciples did a multitude of wrongs. In a matter of moments they broke every rule! Plucking the heads of wheat from the stalks, they "harvested" it; rubbing it between their hands to get the kernels, they "threshed" it; separating the grain from the chaff, they "winnowed" it; and in the process they "prepared a meal"—four forms of work forbidden on the Sabbath.

Now if Sabbath restrictions merely limited one's fun, perhaps they'd be inconsequential and tolerable. But they actually subverted God's intent by making the Sabbath a kind of duty time to keep Him happy. Rather than Sabbath being a special time, a sacred time when God's presence could be better discerned, it became a time when He was kept afar, securely in His judgment seat. Rather than liberating one from hard labor so as to enjoy God's good world, Sabbath had become a prison with walls of time wherein nothing enjoyable could be done. So, while trying to do the good thing of keeping the Sabbath holy, many of Jesus' contemporaries made life miserable for men and women who needed a day of rest. Men and women need a joyous day, but the Pharisees reduced it to a heavy routine of prohibitions.

A New Day for the New Way

Immediately after Pentecost, as soon as Christians began celebrating a new way—Jesus' way—they began celebrating a new day—the Lord's day. Though most of His disciples were Jews, they quickly substituted the Lord's day (Sunday) for the Sabbath (Saturday). "On the first day of the week," Luke says, "we came together to break bread" (Acts 20:7). Accurately speaking, Christians don't observe the Sabbath, the seventh day of the week. Christians celebrate the Lord's day, Sunday, the first day of the week—or the eighth day, as some prefer to say.

Living in the Roman Empire, early Christians faced a society that didn't grant them Sundays off; so Sunday, the Lord's day, was hardly a Jewish-style day of rest. For centuries Christians met (often early in the morning before going about required routines) and rejoiced on the Lord's day, for it helped them remember the Resurrection.

Thus, one of the Apostolic Fathers, Ignatius of Antioch, on his way to Rome to be executed, wrote, "No longer observe the Jewish Sabbaths, but keep holy the Lord's day, on which, through Him and through His death, our life arose."[5] Somewhat later Athanasius, a fourth-century father, noted that Christians kept "no Sabbaths," observing instead "the Lord's Day as a memorial of the beginning of the new creation."[6]

Celebrating creation, old and new, on the first day of the week is the new day for the new way of Christ. Reducing Sunday to "time served," a duty to be grudgingly endured, perverts the good news of Christ's gospel.

I heard a story about a little boy who saw a plaque hanging in his church's foyer, dedicated to the memory of soldiers who had died in the war. He asked, "Who are the people whose names are on the plaque?"

An adult responded, "Those are the names of the men who died in the service."

Instantly interested, the little guy said, "Really? In which service—9:30 or 11:00?"

Admittedly, sometimes our worship services are more dead than alive, more boring than uplifting. But they ought not be. They should celebrate the resurrection of the Lord Jesus. "Jesus is Lord, and He is risen!" That was the motto of the Early Church. So each Sunday believers came together to rejoice, just to be happy in the realization of who Jesus is, to enjoy the reality of His presence. More than anything else, Sunday should be a good time for us, for we know that in Jesus we have entered into eternal life, God's timelessness.

The Lord's day also looks forward to a great day coming, a glorious day when the saints and angels will all be perfected in the ecstasy of heaven. So Sunday, the Lord's day, not only is the first day of the week but also signifies the new creation—the eighth day—that God will establish through Jesus Christ. Each Lord's day we gather to remember joyously His coming—and His coming again.

Key Scripture: Exodus 20:12

Background Scripture:
Micah 7:6; Matthew 5:17;
7:28-29; 10:32-39; 12:46-50;
Mark 10:14; Luke 2:49-51;
John 14:6

*Honor your
father and
your mother.*

CHAPTER 8

THE SANCTITY
OF THE FAMILY

OLD TESTAMENT FOUNDATION: HONOR YOUR
FATHER AND MOTHER

Some of us think our parents are the greatest folks in the world, and we hope to be just like them. Others of us can hardly stand our parents, so we work hard all our life trying to be utterly unlike them. Some of us "sorta" like our folks but wish they would grow up or come down to earth. Some of us couldn't wait to escape the confines of home, to get away from our parents, only to discover quickly we wanted nothing more than to return home, to live in the warmth and shelter the folks provided.

Some of us might be alarmed to know how our folks felt about us! Tensions separating the generations, the generation gap, seem to trouble us forever. Listen to this news item:

> Children now love luxury. They have bad manners, contempt for authority. They show disrespect for

elders and love to talk in place of exercise. Children are now tyrants. . . . They no longer rise when an elder enters the room. They contradict their parents, chatter before company, gobble up food at the table, cross their legs and tyrannize their teachers.

Sound like a letter to today's *Los Angeles Times*? In fact, it's an ancient Greek complaint, recorded 2,400 years ago!

Even earlier, some 2,800 years ago, the prophet Micah cataloged the sins of his contemporaries by crying out, "For a son dishonors his father, a daughter rises up against her mother, a daughter-in-law against her mother-in-law— a man's enemies are the members of his own household" (7:6).

Honestly, we have a problem—a big problem. It's a family problem, a problem with the family. If we're concerned about family, our present and future families, think for a few minutes about God's Word for us: "Honor your father and your mother, so that you may live long in the land the LORD your God is giving you" (Exodus 20:12). The fifth commandment extends God's concern for covenant relationships to the most basic social institution—the family. To live rightly with God, to stay in covenant with Him, we need to live rightly with others, beginning at home.

A Matter of Honor: Appreciation

For the good of the family, children must honor their parents. The word "honor" doesn't necessarily mean a son must like his father, that a daughter must enjoy being around her mother. It's mainly a matter of appreciation, not affection, though there's an incredible amount of natural affection family members share with each other. Yet we must see how it's possible, if necessary, to honor our parents without particularly admiring them.

The fifth commandment means parents deserve something just because they're parents. They're to be honored because of what they've done and the position they occupy, not because they're always effective. We're to honor our parents just because they are our parents, not because they're always the kind of parents we would like them to be. Primarily this means we honor them for giving us the most priceless of all gifts: life.

More than 30 years ago the *Milwaukee Sentinel* conducted a contest titled My Pop's Tops, encouraging children to nominate their dads for the prize. One of the entries said, "Every child should love their father because if it was not for their father where would they be? Nowhere, that's where they'd be. If it was not for fathers you wouldn't see hardly no children around Milwaukee." Our covenant with our parents grows out of the very basic truth that they gave us life. Without them we'd just not *be*.

Some of you were adopted as babies. Naturally you struggle with the decision of your birth mother or parents to give you away. You've wrestled with feelings many of us can never understand. But in the midst of the most powerful feelings, never forget this—it's good to be alive. And your natural mother and father, however else they failed you, gave you life. Some of you may have been abused as children and wrestle with angry, hateful feelings toward your abusive parents. Such feelings are understandable, natural, inevitable. But in the midst of your pain, however much they failed you, there's still, for most of you, an inescapable thankfulness for the gift of life—a gift only parents can give.

Some of you have parents who divorced. You feel divorced as well. You feel what seems to be a depthless ache. To ask you not to feel such pain is like asking a man who has just been stabbed to stop bleeding. Bleeding is a normal response to injury. Your anger, your discontent with your mom and/or dad, is basically a normal, healthy—at least at one stage—response to injury. But amid the pain, always remember this: the most precious gift we've ever received is the gift of life.

So we honor our parents, we appreciate them for who they are, the source of our life. Life is precious, even with its pains. Most of us, however harsh our circumstances, love life and seek to prolong it. We have something to preserve. We're more than nothing, thanks to our parents!

A Necessary Chain of Command: Authority

In honoring our father and mother, we also acknowledge and try to fit into God's plan for creation. We may like democracy, but the universe is no democracy. It's a hierarchy. There's a chain of command, a pyramid of responsibility, built into the very fabric of reality. There is authority derived from God that makes creation harmonious, and parents are commissioned monarchs, ordered to guide their little kingdoms under God's divine direction.

To many of us, "authority" sounds like a dirty word. It has nine letters, so it's too long to be profane! An insightful cartoon portrays some graffiti splashed on a wall, declaring in the first frame, "Question Authority!" The second frame shows a smaller addition: "Says Who?" Good question! For all of us both need and constantly rely upon legitimate authorities.

Too often, of course, we confuse authority with authoritarianism, which is an entirely different issue. A legitimate authority is someone who knows something we need to learn.

I've read every book George Sheehan wrote. He was a medical doctor who was one of the world's elite runners. He knew what makes a good runner. I want to know that. So I read and trust him as an author. He's an authority for me. He would never have wanted to impose his views on me, as would an authoritarian, but he's an authority I choose to heed, for his advice comes with the stamp of wisdom and experience.

So too with Jesus. After He finished the Sermon on the Mount, "the crowds were amazed at his teaching, because he taught as one who had authority, and not as their teachers of the law" (Matthew 7:28-29). Since Jesus wrote the book of human nature, it's understandable that He spoke authoritatively about life. He's no tyrant, no authoritarian, but He's an authority! To know how to live, we find in Jesus "the way, and the truth and the life" (John 14:6).

We need authorities in addition to Jesus, particularly when we're young. We need people who have lived long enough and care deeply enough to help us find our way. So in the family, when it functions as God intended, we find good authority. Better than anyone else, our parents know us. They inscribed our script, for their DNA is literally imprinted in our being. They watched us, more meticulously than anyone else, as we matured. They knew the world we lived in, the world that exerted its influence on us. They witnessed the experiences that helped make us what we are. Honoring our parents means listening to them, following their rules, believing they probably know more than we do, believing they care for us enough to give us good guidance.

In learning to accept our parents' authority, we also learn to accept teachers', preachers', police officers', and presidents' authority. Such folks aren't always right. Now and then they are misguided. They aren't always up-to-date. Still they are usually worth heeding, worth following, because they represent the wisdom of our race, the collective wisdom deeper and surer than our own.

We live in a culture that some observers think is on the verge of ruin. The failure of moms and dads, the divorces and child abuse, the neglect and disinterest have sorely wounded millions of kids. I'd like to reverse or correct all that, but I can't. I have no magic wand, no wonderful formula for the world. Neither have you.

But all of us can, insofar as possible, begin trying to rebuild the families we're part of. Even those of us who are not parents are children. So we can, each of us, do something about the family. That something begins with learning how to rightly honor, to esteem, our fathers and our mothers and to submit to legitimate authorities as we encounter and live with them as God intended.

NEW TESTAMENT INTERNALIZATION: DOING OUR FATHER'S BUSINESS

Years ago I heard James Dobson tell a story about sitting with a group of strangers in a meeting. The time came for a coffee break, and the leader of the group asked one member if he wanted to break for coffee and doughnuts. Insecure, the guy played it safe and said, "No, not now." Then the leader went around the room, asking each individual if he or she wanted a break. At last he came to Dobson, who said enthusiastically, "I sure do." Moving toward the refreshments, he found the rest of the group instantly at his heels, grateful for the break from the lecture. They couldn't wait for the break they had all declined![1]

Sometimes it takes courage to stand up and act according to what you believe—even if you want no more than a cup of coffee. Most of us, most of the time, conform to the crowd around us. Even the most individualistic of us tends to dress like others our age. So I often wonder, Have any of us the courage to stand up and be counted for what counts? Have any of us dared to stand alone, doing what's right regardless of what it might cost? The truth is, if we want to follow Jesus, we'll often have to stand up and defy those who discourage us from discipleship. That means at times doing what our peers, and even our parents, disapprove of.

Discipline Demands Decisions

Any decision demands discipline. And decisions determine destiny. So decisions flowing from discipline really matter. They determine if what we do ultimately matters.

Though we honor our parents, sometimes in following Jesus we must make decisions that disappoint them, decisions that take us in directions they can't understand. In Luke's Gospel, Jesus' first recorded decision disappointed His parents. Joseph and Mary took Jesus to Jerusalem for the Passover Feast, and as they returned to Nazareth, they discovered He wasn't with the extended family. They returned to Jerusalem, where He was found sitting in the Temple discussing theology and amazing His elders. His "astonished" parents chastised Him for causing them distress. In response, Jesus said, "Why were you searching for me? . . . Didn't you know I had to be in my Father's house?" (2:49). Or in the words of the King James Version, "Wist ye not that I must be about my Father's business?"

On one level Jesus may have been saying to His parents, "Why are you so upset? You know Me well enough to know that I would be in the Temple. You should have looked for Me here." On another level it is clear that Jesus was making a statement that showed His parents (and us) that He was aware of His divine connection with God. This is a preview of His later teachings as an adult that doing the will of God is more important than any other relationship. (See Luke 8:19-21.)

Jesus' parents did not understand the full meaning of His statement. Yet, Jesus submitted to their earthly authority over Him until His time and calling would be fulfilled as an adult. "But they did not understand what he was saying to them. Then he went down to Nazareth with them and was *obedient to them*" (2:50-51, emphasis added).

"Nothing is more difficult, and therefore more precious," said Napoléon, "than to be able to decide."[2] He was right. We're routinely paralyzed by uncertainty, doubt, fear. Given the chance, we'll call for more study, refer the issue to a committee, and hope someone else decides for us. To decide, to make a choice and follow it, takes self-discipline, and disciplined choices may separate us from others—even our parents.

For a Christian, as one has said, "One thing is clear:

we understand Christ only if we commit ourselves to him in a stark 'Either-Or.' He did not go to the cross to ornament and embellish our life."[3] Too often we would like to add Jesus to our life, like wood filler when finishing furniture, just to smooth out the cracks on the surface. But Jesus is not an add-on luxury. Indeed, "We are concerned with Christ and nothing else. Let Christ be Christ."[4] Still more: "In Jesus God has said Yes and Amen to it all, and that Yes and Amen is the firm ground on which we stand."[5]

Discipline Demands Determination

The discipline that discipleship demands roots itself in a determination to do God's will. In Matthew's Gospel Jesus said:

> Whoever acknowledges me before men, I will also acknowledge him before my Father in heaven. But whoever disowns me before men, I will disown him before my Father in heaven.
>
> Do not suppose that I have come to bring peace to the earth. I did not come to bring peace, but a sword. For I have come to turn "a man against his father, a daughter against her mother, a daughter-in-law against her mother-in-law—a man's enemies will be the members of his own household."
>
> Anyone who loves his father or mother more than me is not worthy of me; . . . and anyone who does not take his cross and follow me is not worthy of me. Whoever finds his life will lose it, and whoever loses his life for my sake will find it (10:32-39).

The good life Christ provides involves discipline. In fact, I sometimes suspect self-discipline is the one thing necessary to live well. With it we can make it; without it we'll slip and slide from side to side, never really doing anything of substance.

Sophocles wrote long ago in *Antigone*, "If men live decently it is because discipline saves their very lives for them."[6] More recently Tom Landry, the former football coach of the Dallas Cowboys, said it this way: "My job is to get men to do what they don't want to do so that they can achieve what they always wanted to achieve."

Most of us know that the difference between a child and an adult boils down to this: Adults do what's worthwhile, knowing that work, though difficult, must be done in order to live well. Children do what's pleasing, always trying to evade the difficult or uncomfortable.

Making fun life's goal veils the sorrow of not doing anything substantial, and when we're too young to be able to do much, there's little inner satisfaction. So we naturally, quite normally, seek to have fun. What we really need, what we deeply long for, is to know we are in fact competent, able to do good things well.

That, incidentally, is why children need, more than most anything other than love, daily chores. No healthy kid wants to do chores, but kids need them more than they know. One of the ultimate cruelties parents lay on their kids is to let them play all day, every day. For it's only when we learn the value of routine and worthwhile work that we begin to understand and appreciate the fuller joys of creativity.

Real joy, genuine satisfaction, we find, comes from doing something substantial. Being amused, wanting to have fun, leaves us empty, lacking substance. But giving ourselves to something, expending our energies, concretely accomplishing something lifts us up, gives us a zest for life. It isn't always pleasant, but it's worthwhile.

Jesus calls us to be disciples, to take the road less traveled, because "he knows that his mission is a rugged minority movement, a tough, divisive affair, and he prefers to make this clear rather than give false hope."[7]

Discipline Determines Destinies

I've been thinking about the fact that though Jesus

loved children, though He said, "Let the little children come to me, and do not hinder them, for the kingdom of God belongs to such as these" (Mark 10:14), He never opened a Sunday School. He didn't gather a group of kids for a backyard Bible study. He seemed uninterested in youth ministry. He sought out young men, but they were mature young men who could do the work of living and proclaiming His gospel.

Consequently, these young men belonged to "the company of the committed." They who follow Jesus find family ties in the family of God more precious than in any human family. In Matthew 12:46-50, we read:

> While Jesus was still talking to the crowd, . . . Someone told him, "Your mother and brothers are standing outside, wanting to speak to you."
>
> He replied to him, "Who is my mother, and who are my brothers?" Pointing to his disciples, he said, "Here are my mother and my brothers. For whoever does the will of my Father in heaven is my brother and sister and mother."

Clearly, Jesus calls us to make decisions, disciplined decisions, that characterize disciples, and it's disciples who join Jesus in living out the way of life God has designed for us.

A century ago Dwight L. Moody preached a series of messages for a group of college students at a retreat center. Also present was a missionary who urged young people to respond to the challenge of world missions. At the end of the retreat, exactly 100 young collegians committed themselves to full-time missionary service. In a few months they returned to their colleges and shared the joy of their decision. In a brief period of time some 5,000 young persons, the corps of the Student Volunteer Movement, the best and brightest of their generation, gave themselves to spreading the good news of Jesus throughout the world. As a result of their courage and work, today there are growing Christian churches in places such as Korea, China, and Africa. They made a difference, an eternal difference, in the lives of millions of people. They made critical decisions.[8]

Decisions demand discipline, and discipline determines destinies. And our ultimate obedience is to our Heavenly Father; our ultimate allegiance to His kingdom, rather than our biological families.

Key Scripture: Exodus 20:13

Background Scripture:
Genesis 4:6-9; 9:5-6;
Deuteronomy 19:10;
Matthew 5:21-22; 7:1

*You shall
not murder.*

CHAPTER 9

THE SANCTITY OF LIFE

OLD TESTAMENT FOUNDATION: DO NOT MURDER

One of the stars of the United States' 1992 Olympic basketball "dream team," Charles Barkley, in talking to a reporter in Barcelona during the games, insisted that Spain was nice but that he really missed the United States.

"I miss America," he said. "I miss crime and murder. I miss Philadelphia. There hasn't been a brutal stabbing or anything here in the last 24 hours. I've missed it."

There's heavy irony in Barkley's words, of course. Lots of us love America, but it's a land awash with bloodshed.

In America since 1900 some 10,000 people a year have been murdered—a century's total of a million or so. Babies born in the 1970s were more likely to be murdered than American soldiers killed in World War II. In America young males are 20 times as likely to be murdered as their European counterparts, 40 times as likely as their Japanese peers.

Folks kill folks. And they always have, long before

America was settled. If you're interested in gory details, the historical record provides them. Centuries ago a Hungarian countess, Erszebet Bathory (1560-1614), was accused of killing 610 young girls, the names of whom she carefully recorded in her notebook. A bit earlier a Chinese named Chang Hsien-Chung seized control of the province of Szechwan, where in 5 years he killed 40 million people, including 280 of his own wives! We are, it seems, born killers.

Whether we study the newspapers, history books, or our own experiences, we should conclude that our society is violent because we (you and I) are by nature capable of violence. Like an automobile's tempered spring, we're inflexibly bent toward it. At all times, in all places, earth has been dyed red with blood. Day after day, year after year, the killing goes on.

How long will it take, we wonder, to stop the killing? How long will we go on murdering? Quite frankly, unlike those who display bumper stickers urging us to "visualize world peace," we'll never abolish violence. It's simply a part of the crimson bent toward evil ingrained in our sinful nature. Despite that, the Bible calls those of us who want to live with God into a covenant relationship with Him, which makes it clear, in the words of the sixth commandment, "You shall not murder" (Exodus 20:13).

The Crime Defined: An Anatomy of Murder

The Hebrew word used in this commandment appears only 40 times in the Old Testament. It clearly condemns deliberately taking an innocent person's life—what the law labels murder. Other words are used for killing or causing death, such as what happens in self-defense, police action, or just war.

What concerns us here is that "innocent blood will not be shed" (Deuteronomy 19:10). With this in mind, at least five kinds of killing—the deliberate taking of innocent life—are forbidden: premeditated murder, abortion, mercy killing, unjust war, and suicide. Let's consider the first of these life-and-death issues—premeditated murder—for it's the starting point for the others.

Most clearly, Scripture condemns first-degree, premeditated murder. To study an anatomy of a murder, turn to the beginning of human history, recorded in Genesis, where we read the story of Cain killing Abel. The first step in the making of a murderer begins when Cain turns away from God. The text doesn't indicate the precise problem, but it's evident that Cain wanted to do things his way rather than God's.

Abel offered God his best, but Cain seems to have grabbed a couple of apples and a handful of wheat and insisted that God accept whatever he presented. It's like a man who has asked a woman to a fancy banquet (where all the women will wear nice corsages) and picks some dandelions and eucalyptus leaves, ties them together with a shoestring, and expects her to be impressed with his gift.

Cain stepped away from the Lord, and the next step led him to shift his focus to himself and his own interests, languishing in self-pity because the Lord failed to accept his substitute offering. Hardly anything is more pathetic than a "pity party," but lots of us regularly throw them! Cain pouted. His face was "downcast" with a pout cloud.

In that condition he opened his mind and heart to sin. The Scripture reads, "Then the LORD said to Cain, 'Why are you angry? Why is your face downcast? If you do what is right, will you not be accepted? But if you do not do what is right, sin is crouching at your door; it desires to have you, but you must master it" (Genesis 4:6-7).

Cain chose to do wrong. Having turned away from God, having turned his attention to himself and his grievance, he then turned against his brother. He crafted a plan. He envisioned a way to entice, entrap, and eliminate his brother. He premeditated murder. Whatever the ruse, as soon as they were alone, "Cain attacked his brother Abel and killed him" (v. 8). He turned on his brother with evil intent. He killed.

The deed done, Cain next switched off his conscience. He evaded God's question, "Where is your brother Abel?" (v. 9).

"How should I know?" he seemed to mean when he said, "Am I my brother's keeper?" (v. 9). Perhaps he tried to lie by saying, "Abel's probably playing in the fields, practicing his spear throwing. Why, he's so reckless he may spear himself one of these days." But the truth was that Cain had murdered Abel and couldn't evade God's judgment.

Covenant Commitment: Revere Life

There are many ramifications to the prohibition "You shall not murder" (Exodus 20:13). But more important for the people of God is the positive proposition underlying the commandment—living with the Lord of life enables us to rejoice in the beauty of life and to join God in preserving it. Underlying the prohibition is an injunction—celebrate the sanctity of life, for human life is even more than sacred, it's hallowed and precious because it's God's gift to us.

That ancient reverence for human life, rooted in the very will of God, stands revealed in God's covenant with Noah immediately after the Flood. It's recorded in one of the most illuminating passages in God's Word: "And from each man, too, I will demand an accounting for the life of his fellow man. Whoever sheds the blood of man, by man shall his blood be shed; for in the image of God has God made man" (Genesis 9:5-6).

Then God sketched a rainbow in the sky, an eternally recurring sign of His covenant, binding himself to us and all living creatures. Life's a gift, very sacred, and we must treasure it. In the words of an African proverb, "Human blood is heavy; the man who has shed it cannot run away."

Gifts are important. Years ago I spoke for a Native American youth camp. At the end of the week a Comanche friend gave me a ring as a token of friendship. It was too big for me, and when I got home, my wife asked what I planned to do with the ring. She suggested she might like to wear it on a chain as a necklace, so I gave it to her.

The next year, somewhat unexpectedly, I spoke for the same camp. When I met my friend, he asked, "Where's your ring?" (I confess I really wanted to lie a little at that point!) I told him the truth: I'd given it to my wife. He then informed me that if I wanted to give my wife a ring, I should buy one from him for her. He had given me the ring as an act of friendship. I agreed. I ordered a ring for her and paid for it. Then I went home, took back my ring, had it reduced to fit my finger, and now treasure it as a reminder of a generous act. It's a gift worth preserving.

Even more important, we've been given a gift of life, a precious gift from the Lord and Giver of life. I deeply appreciate the gift. So do you! So I urge you to join me, to join the Lord above, in treasuring the gift of life—upholding God's covenant with Noah, inscribed in the sixth commandment, refusing to take from others what God has given them.

NEW TESTAMENT INTERNALIZATION: NURSE NO ANGER

Do you ever wonder about the amount of anger that seethes like a pressure cooker all around us? There's lots of anger surging across our culture. It's an anger that often looks as if it could kill. And if looks could kill, there'd be lots of dead bodies littering the land!

There's anger etched into the faces of various protesters—I'm amazed by the hateful expressions on both abortion rights and antiabortion advocates as they march in the streets, shouting and even hurling things to vent their convictions. There's anger inscribed in the lyrics of rock and rap singers who venomously attack a world they apparently find hostile.

There's anger in our communities. A few years ago I was walking along a street near my home and saw an elderly man chasing a handful of junior high boys who were on rollerblades. He had a steel rod in his hand and hurled it at them. It missed and clattered down the street. Then one of the boys picked up the rod and took off after the man, who hustled back up the street. The boy tossed the rod and also missed. Then the man and his wife came back toward the boys. At that point I intervened and tried to cool things down. Mainly I tried to talk with the boys, who seemed to be the antagonists in the altercation, but I did little more than give both sides time to cool down. It seems the boys played pranks and had otherwise irritated the elderly couple. Finally the man got so mad he resorted to rod throwing. That's dangerous! It even bordered on the ridiculous. But it illustrates how anger gets explosive.

Is there any solution? We can pass laws to punish murder, but have we no way to wash out the anger that wells up in the hearts of murderers? There's only one solution I know—the Jesus solution. Jesus said, deepening the Old Testament's prohibition of murder: "You have heard that it was said to the people long ago, 'Do not murder, and anyone who murders will be subject to judgment.' But I tell you that anyone who is *angry* with his brother will be subject to judgment" (Matthew 5:21-22, emphasis added).

Nurse No Grudges! Renounce Revenge!

Rooted in Jesus' statement, Christian thinkers have identified anger as one of the seven deadly sins, one of the sins that surely separates us from God. It's important to understand that the anger condemned is not a passing emotion, not a hurt feeling, but a harboring of the will for revenge, a nursing of a grudge.

There are two Greek words for "anger." One, *thumos,*

describes the rapid, explosive emotion that responds to injury or injustice.

When someone sticks a knife into my back, I bleed. That's a normal, healthy reaction to the injury. When someone attacks us, physically or verbally, we feel anger. That's a normal, healthy reaction to assault. We might prefer not to bleed, we might be embarrassed by the bloody mess we make, but we'll bleed. If someone hits me in the chest, I'll probably not say, "Oh, thanks. I needed that. Kinda makes my day." No, I'll feel anger.

The other kind of anger, *orgē,* means a lasting, furious, vengeful desire to see an enemy suffer. Though the phrase "without a cause" (Matthew 5:22, KJV) is not found in the best Greek manuscripts, both John Chrysostom and Augustine, who were preaching at the end of the fourth century, used versions that included the clause, for it seemed to them the anger Jesus condemned needed to be clearly understood as a will to vengeance rather than an emotional reaction. As a modern commentator says, the Greek phrase "literally means 'is being angry,' 'bears anger,' 'carries anger,' or in our idiom, 'nurses a grudge.'"[1]

This kind of anger is succinctly phrased in the motto some folks live by: "Don't get angry—get even." A prominent Spanish general and statesman, Ramón María Narváez, lay dying in 1869. A priest asked him, "Does Your Excellency forgive all your enemies?" Replied Narváez, "I do not have to forgive my enemies. I have had them all shot."[2] Now that's a graphic way to get even!

It is, in fact, difficult if not impossible to get even. We usually do more harm to ourselves than to our enemies when we try to right the scales of justice. Consider the case of a woman who came to Ibn Saud, the first king of Saudi Arabia, in 1932. She approached the king, seeking to have the man who had killed her husband executed.

It seems the accused man had been gathering dates in a palm tree, slipped, and fell on her husband, fatally injuring him. So the king asked if the fall had been deliberate. Were the two men enemies? Apparently they didn't know each other, and the fall was purely accidental. But the widow demanded revenge: life for life.

Ibn Saud tried to reason with her, urging her to accept a cash settlement or something else. But she demanded a life for a life. Finally the king relented. He said, "It is your right to exact compensation, and it is also your right to ask for this man's life. But it is my right to decree how he shall die. You shall take this man with you, and he shall be tied to the foot of a palm tree, and then you yourself shall climb to the top of the tree and cast yourself down upon him from that height. In that way you will take his life as he took your husband's."

There was a long pause. "Or perhaps," Ibn Saud added, "you would prefer after all to take the blood money?" The widow wisely took the money.[3]

Call No One "Stupid"! Avoid Put-downs!

Having warned against nursing a grudge, Jesus continued, "Again, anyone who says to his brother, 'Raca,' is answerable to the Sanhedrin" (Matthew 5:22). Not only are we to forsake revenge, but also we're to avoid lashing out at people, calling them names, saying things such as "Raca," which means "You idiot," "Stupid," "Dum-dum." How often we say, with words, looks, and intonations, "Oh, you stupid you!" That's raca. For raca reflects contempt for another person, the attitude that he or she is somehow second-class, unworthy of respect.

We say raca more by the tone of our voice, the looks that accompany our speech, than by code words of some sort. Now and then my wife rebukes me (reminding me how clearly we communicate without words) by saying, "You're giving me that 'Oh, you stupid you' look." One of my friends once applied a biblical phrase to me, saying, "Gerard doesn't 'suffer fools gladly'" (2 Corinthians 11:19,

KJV). And I took it as a rebuke, not a compliment. I need to know I have the tendency, the ability, to put down folks who are not on my wavelength, who fail to measure up to whatever standard I'm using.

When King James I ruled England, a less-than-notable envoy appeared in court. Later the king asked Francis Bacon what he thought of the marquess.

"Your Majesty," Bacon said, "people of such dimensions are like four- or five-story houses; the upper rooms are the most poorly furnished."[4]

So we say, "She's an airhead," or, "He's not running on all cylinders." Is that not part of raca Jesus had in mind?

Call No One "Fool"! Cease Condemning

Still more: Jesus said, "Anyone who says, 'You fool!' will be in danger of the fire of hell" (Matthew 5:22). Whereas "raca" means "stupid," the word "fool" refers to a person's moral character. We call someone a fool when we malign his or her good name, when we destroy his or her reputation as a person of moral integrity. To call a person a scoundrel, to label a person a no-good, is to seek to take God's place in judging—and damning—persons. We're told, "Do not judge, or you too will be judged" (7:1).

Over a century ago Henry Ward Beecher was one of the most prominent men in America. Weekly he preached to thousands in New York City's Plymouth Church. One Sunday he arrived and found a letter to him containing one word: "Fool." He told the people about it that day, adding, "I have known many an instance of a man writing a letter and forgetting to sign his name, but this is the only instance I have ever known of a man signing his name and forgetting to write the letter."[5] Would that all of us could respond to criticism and condemnation with Beecher's humor. Yet even humor cannot undo the harm done by harsh words, critical comments, and malicious gossip.

Certainly we are creatures with language. We use

words. Some of us use them incessantly. Jesus said there are folks with eyes who see not and folks with ears who hear not. He never said there are folks with tongues that speak not. We certainly keep our mouths in motion. Lots of us are, to tell the truth, motormouths. And many of our tongues seem to run fastest when our brains are idling. Perhaps speaking for lots of old-timers, an elderly man said, "Many of us are like a pair of old shoes—all worn-out but the tongue." In my observation, tongues rarely wear out.

The Jewish Talmud tells of a king who sent two of his court jesters on a mission. "Foolish Simon," the king said, "go and bring back the best thing in the world. And you, Silly John, go and find me the worst thing in the world." Both jesters quickly departed and almost as quickly returned with a package. Simon bowed before the king, saying, "Behold, Sire, the best thing in the world." His package contained a human tongue. Silly John then snickered and undid his package, saying, "The worst thing in the world, Sire!" Another human tongue!

So we've been given the best and the worst thing in the world—a tongue. The question today for me is this— how will I use it? To walk with Jesus, to talk as Jesus talks, means to let His love, present in the power of His Holy Spirit, free us from resentment and deliver us from the temptation to use our tongues as weapons of destruction. When we think about controlling the tongue, it seems humanly impossible. And it is. Only the new covenant, whereby God has promised to put His law in our hearts, enables us to speak in a Christlike manner.

When we think about what Jesus says, most of us are driven to despair of ever doing what He urges. How can anyone live like this? That's precisely what He wants us to discover. On our own we never will. Immediately before this passage, He said that "unless your righteousness surpasses that of the Pharisees and the teachers of the law, you will certainly not enter the kingdom of heaven" (Matthew 5:20).

So how are we to get in? Only by His gracious assistance. To live as Jesus wants us to, we must learn, as did Brother Lawrence, that "when an occasion of practicing some virtue was offered, he addressed himself to God, saying, 'Lord, I cannot do this unless thou enablest me;' and that then he received strength more than sufficient."

Key Scripture: Exodus 20:14

Background Scripture: Proverbs 5:15; 1 Thessalonians 4:1-7; 1 John 2:15-17

You shall not commit adultery.

CHAPTER 10

THE SANCTITY OF SEX

OLD TESTAMENT FOUNDATION: ADULTERY? NO!

"Jack and Elaine Kirschke were nothing if not adult about adultery," began a *Time* magazine article years ago. "He liked women and she liked men, and neither was a spoilsport. There was only one house rule for their not-quite-home on voguish Rivo Alto Canal in Naples, California: when one party had the pad, the other stayed away."[1]

Married for 24 years, both were prosperous professionals (she, a fashion designer; he, a chief prosecutor for the Los Angeles district attorney), good-looking, and "cool." They had it all together—until Jack killed Elaine and her latest lover. Sometimes we're not as "adult about adultery" as we pretend.

But we certainly keep on doing it. In *The Day America Told the Truth,* one chapter is titled "Infidelity: It's Rampant."[2] Almost one-third of married Americans have had or are having affairs. According to researchers, "The majority of Americans (62 percent) think that there's nothing morally wrong with the affairs they're having. Once again, we hear the killer rationalization that 'everybody does it too.'" Interestingly enough, however, these adulterers themselves do not think their spouses are the "everybodies" doing it.[3] Somehow spouses of adulterers are supposed to be faithful to their unfaithful partners.

These are recent illustrations, but actually adultery is as old as the human race. With some justification, prostitution has been called the oldest profession, for if human sinfulness is evident anywhere, it's in our disordered sexual conduct—to which Scripture simply says, in the words of the seventh commandment, "You shall not commit adultery" (Exodus 20:14). This commandment, like the others, is easy to understand. It is, however, as history reveals, terribly difficult to follow.

Infidelity Is Always a Threat

Our world is full of temptations. We struggle daily with them. While they come in diverse forms, the world abounds with sexual tempters. Too many folks live by the "Zsa Zsa" rule. Zsa Zsa Gabor, as you know, is an oft-married Hollywood film star. A magazine writer once asked her, as well as some other prominent women, "What is the first thing you notice about a woman?"

"Her way of speaking," was mystery writer Agatha Christie's answer.

"Her hands," said Maria Callas, the opera singer.

With unusual candor, Zsa Zsa declared, "Her husband."[4] Whether true or not, such stories illustrate the Hollywood ethos that thoroughly pervades our society.

Temptations, when embraced, bring little but grief and sorrow. In the short run they're exciting, but in the long run they're as devastating as a spring flood. Adultery is so insidious because it so easily destroys what's most precious. If I were to bring $1 million into a room and begin burning the money, folks nearby would protest. It's just wrong to waste something that's precious. If I brought

Leonardo's *Mona Lisa* into a shopping mall and started shredding it with a knife, I imagine someone would physically restrain me. It's demonstrably wrong to destroy a precious work of art. Similarly, marriage is precious, and it's wrong to destroy it.

Yet millions of folks argue that it's fine to sleep around. Of course, they say it's acceptable only as long as the folks involved are "consenting adults," as long as "no one gets hurt." Whatever their married estate, there's nothing to worry about as long as everyone involved gets some satisfaction, they say.

But let me argue that someone always gets hurt. Whenever I donate blood at the blood bank, I'm reminded, as I answer the seemingly endless questions about my sexual contacts, that folks who need blood need good blood. I'm reminded of the thousands of innocent hemophiliacs who are dying because their blood transfusions were tainted with the AIDS virus. Some folks claim to think monogamy is obsolete, unnecessary, irrelevant. But they'll not be welcome at the blood bank.

Good blood comes from right living. Good marriages come with right living as well. Even more: Keeping marriage vows builds spiritual integrity. The integrity we inwardly hunger for comes with sustained commitment to a lasting, loving relationship with our spouse. Adultery, in Scripture, means infidelity to one's husband or wife. What's wrong with adultery is not merely the pleasure of promiscuous sex—it's the breaking of vows, the breaking of solemn promises. It's forbidden because we're called to be covenant-keeping people. Keeping promises keeps us human. Few things more clearly mark a fundamentally good person than his or her faithfulness.

Marriage Matters, for Vows Validate Integrity

The spirituality of sex can be sustained only within long-term monogamous relationships. Since adultery annihilates such relationships, the Bible insists that we not commit adultery. For adultery not only disrupts human bonds but also distances us from God. In committing adultery, we turn away from God, rejecting His Lordship over all realms of existence.

Fidelity! Faithfulness! Nothing means more to a person than staying true to the vows he or she has made to a person. I read that the late Princess Diana and Prince Charles of England began to have difficulties with their marriage on their honeymoon. It seems the prince actually wore a ring, composed of two strands of interwoven gold, that had been given him by one of his former flames. How cruel! How difficult it would be for any woman—Princess Di included—to know her husband still cherished someone other than her.

If you study English history, you know that the royal family has had its share of philanderers. In 1910 King Edward VII died. He was a notorious adulterer, forcing his wife, Alexandra, a Danish princess, to pretend she didn't see what all the world knew. When her husband died, Alexandra was momentarily grief-stricken, but then she brightened up and, with a sense of humor, said, "Now at least I know where he is."

The Bible calls us to a better way. Thus, the guiding assumption of the Old Testament is this: sex and marriage are good when they're kept sacred by fidelity.

Years ago Alex Comfort published a best-seller titled *The Joy of Sex*, which was basically a how-to manual. The book might better have been titled "The Pleasures of Sex," but Comfort picked the right title, for there's a deep joy to a lasting sexual bond that helps unite persons who deeply love one another. We're not to commit adultery, because marriage can be so good. There's nothing sweeter than sex in marriage. There's nothing better than drinking "water from your own cistern" (Proverbs 5:15). Some of our grandparents, some of our great-grandparents have been married for decades. If we want to know something about the "joy of sex," we'd be wise to follow their example rather than that of the Hollywood stars who jump from bed to bed.

There is, in fact, a joy to sex that transcends its fun. The joy of sex comes when two persons trust each other enough to enjoy the real intimacy that comes from living together, sharing life together. It's what Martin Luther wisely described when he said, "Let the wife make her husband glad to come home, and let him make her sorry to see him leave."

NEW TESTAMENT INTERNALIZATION: CHASTITY? YES!

Many of us would like to be Christians; indeed, many of us readily identify ourselves as Christians. In fact, a 1992 survey revealed that 80 percent of the American populace claim to be Christian. But we're not too sure what that means. There are lots of definitions. Some have simply said yes to a presentation of the Four Spiritual Laws. Others have joined a church. Some remember a special feeling, an exhilarating experience years ago.

Let me state that to be a Christian means living a life that pleases God, a life sanctified by God's Spirit, who enables us truly to love God. To all who want to be Christian, let me remind you of the wisdom of the ancient Church. In the early centuries, the best thinkers of the Church set forth the "evangelical counsels," some ways of pursuing spiritual perfection—chastity, simplicity, humility. Clearly rooted in Jesus' wilderness temptations, they find concise expression in the words of the Beloved Disciple, John, who said:

Do not love the world or anything in the world. If anyone loves the world, the love of the Father is not in him. For everything in the world—the cravings of sinful man, the lust of his eyes and the boasting of what he has and does—comes not from the Father but from

the world. The world and its desires pass away, but
the man who does the will of God lives forever *(1 John
2:15-17)*.

To live with God means to handle sex, money, and
power rightly. Right now let's consider sex, using a passage from 1 Thessalonians as our guide. This is probably
Paul's first letter, written from Corinth in A.D. 51. He had
just been in Thessalonica and wrote to remind the young
church of the basics of the Christian faith. In the first three
chapters he stressed doctrinal essentials. In the fourth
chapter he turned practical, telling them "how to live in order to please God" (v. 1).

It is God's will that you should be sanctified: that
you should avoid sexual immorality; that each of you
should learn to control his own body in a way that is
holy and honorable, not in passionate lust like the hea-
then, who do not know God; and that in this matter
no one should wrong his brother or take advantage of
him. The Lord will punish men for all such sins, as we
have already told you and warned you. For God did
not call us to be impure, but to live a holy life *(vv. 3-7)*.

Abstain from Fornication!

To follow the Holy Spirit's direction, according to the
above text, means we "avoid sexual immorality," that we
"abstain from fornication" (KJV). There's a sexual dimension to sanctification, a sexual tone to the good life. One of
the main themes that unites all of Scripture is faithfulness
to the covenant. As a central theme in the Bible, faithfulness is best illustrated by marriage, the model of promise
keeping.

In Albert Camus's *The Fall,* an insightful atheist
lamented, "I sometimes think of what future historians
will say of us. A single sentence will suffice for modern
man: he fornicated and read the papers."[5]

That pretty much sums it up! Modernity celebrates

sexuality and propaganda. In response, Christians need to bear witness to their faith by refusing to accept the modern mood. Simply saying no to illicit sex is part of the Christian ethic. Paul wrote to believers surrounded by sexual promiscuity, a world much like modern culture, and they needed to know why to say no to fornication.

For our own good we need to know when to say no, and we need to know why it's often good to say so. Let me suggest some reasons why I think chastity, a pro-abstinence stance, makes sense as well as follows the biblical principle.

First, saying no is good for one's body. Chastity, restricting sexual activity to marriage, keeps us physically healthy. There's no better way to prevent unwanted pregnancy and sexually transmitted diseases.

Second, say no for the good of your soul. Abstinence keeps us emotionally healthy. It protects us from feelings of guilt and of being used and abandoned, feelings that too often follow fornication. However well we fake it, we hurt when we're sexually manipulated. One thing that makes us uniquely human is our guilt feelings. Dogs and cats live perfectly carefree sex lives, "doing it" whenever and with whomever they feel like. But they apparently have no sense of even passing attachment to their partner in pleasure. We're not dogs and cats, however, even though it seems we easily ape their behavior.

Be Holy, Wholly Spirit-filled

Along with the "Just say no" emphasis of this passage, however, there's a positive theme, the important message of God's will for our good, which is basic to Christian life. If we abstain from fornication, we will find the good life, the holy life, the sanctified life, for which we're designed.

It's good, for one thing, to learn self-control. Self-discipline is basically what separates the men from the boys, the women from the girls. I really admire men like Art

Monk, a professional football player. For years he played for the Washington Redskins, and as an older man he managed to keep up with his younger teammates. He pursued perfection as a football player, joining his teammates for lunch but munching an apple while they inhaled cheeseburgers and fries. He lived a disciplined life, and he gained the rewards as a football star.

That's truth for life. We must submit to discipline in order to learn self-discipline in order to live as we really want to live. Folks who drift through life, doing what comes naturally whenever possible with whoever's around, never grow up. They're perpetual adolescents, controlled by their glands, never really free to be mature persons. But when we learn to control our bodies, we gain maturity, realizing what it means to be fully human, fully alive—wholly human, holy with life.

Still more: it's good to have moral borders, to respect legitimate sexual boundaries. That's because what we most deeply desire is not sexual pleasure but sexual intimacy, the kind of intimacy that's more than momentary sex, the kind of intimacy that thoroughly binds together two persons.[6] But what we lack all too often is the courage to reveal our inner self so as to establish real intimacy.

A woman wrote to Dear Abby complaining that she had been on the pill for two years while living with her boyfriend and thought he should pay half of the prescription bill—but she didn't feel she knew him well enough to discuss money! As one teenage woman confessed, "It is far easier to 'bare your bottom' than to 'bare your soul.'"[7]

But we must bare our souls to establish intimate personal relationships. There must be heart-to-heart truth at the heart of lasting, intimate unions. And that's exactly what the Bible teaches: Fidelity makes us happy. The Bible's "restrictions concerning sexuality," says one rabbi, "are not negative; they allow human passion, human sexuality to be a place of holiness. By saying 'no' to the wrong situation we create the 'yes' to the right emotion. That's the definition of marriage: permissible, holy passion to which we say 'yes,' and it does not violate our dwelling place."[8]

God would like for us to know the joy of holy living. That's why Jesus insisted we not lust for illicit sexual liaisons. He taught us to avoid lust because we're to live in the truth, and there's no truth in lust, for lust lies.

Key Scripture: Exodus 20:15

Background Scripture:
1 Kings 21:3-7; Ephesians
4:28; Philippians 3:5;
2 Thessalonians 3:6-10

You shall not steal.

CHAPTER 11

THE SANCTITY OF PROPERTY

OLD TESTAMENT FOUNDATION: DO NOT STEAL

Years ago my wife and I built a log home on eight acres in a beautiful valley in eastern Kansas. It was secluded and, consequently, vulnerable. One day during the first week of the school term, when both of us were away teaching, a burglar broke in and ransacked the place, looking for our hidden treasures. He dumped out all the drawers to see if we had stashed some cash. (Of ultimate insult to my wife, he dumped out her jewelry drawers—and took nothing!) He stole a 35 mm camera with lenses, which my father had given me, but that was all he found worth taking.

Now the financial value of what he took—especially since insurance covered much of the loss—was not terribly significant. The hours I had to spend repairing the door he crowbarred open were not all that precious. But the personal assault, the sense of being violated, endured. He stole more than a camera—he injured us! He made our world less safe, less homelike, less what it ought to be.

104

So I endorse the eighth commandment: "You shall not steal" (Exodus 20:15). The Hebrew word used, *ganab*, simply means "to take that which belongs to another without his or her consent or knowledge." Simple enough. None of us want people to steal our stuff. But, manifestly, they do. And folks do it in a variety of ways, ranging from force to fraud.

By Force

Thieves—bank robbers, muggers, burglars—simply take what they want by force. I heard about one bank robber who parked his car near the bank and left the engine running so as to expedite his getaway. An elderly lady noted the idling car, removed the keys, and locked it; then she followed the young man into the bank. While he was at the teller's window demanding cash, the lady tapped him on the shoulder and said, "Sonny, you should never leave your keys in the car. Someone might steal it." Sufficiently flustered, he grabbed the keys and fled the bank.

Another bank robber hit the same bank three times. An FBI agent, talking to the teller after the last incident, said, "Did you notice anything special about the robber?"

"Yes," said the teller. "He seemed to be better dressed each time."

Such incidents, though perhaps humorous, remind us how routinely people steal by force, openly taking what's rightfully someone else's property. Clearly the Bible, as well as the civil law and common conscience, condemns this.

By Petty Theft

Few of us, I suppose, will engage in bank robbery or armed burglary. Most of us fear the police and prison sufficiently to refuse even to contemplate such acts. But ordinary persons are tempted to take what doesn't belong to them while shopping or on the job. Shoplifting statistics reveal that each year there are some 175 million incidents—equal to more than half the people in the United States. This is not to say over half the folks are shoplifting, of course, for some offenders commit scores of offenses—far more than their fair share. Amazingly, most shoplifters are middle-class people who don't need what they steal. They are driven to get something for nothing, seemingly inspired by the old hymn to "steal away, steal away"!

Then there are those who steal from their employers. Some stores write off as much as 50 percent of their profits to "inventory shrinkage." Employees, some analysts think, take three times as much merchandise as do shoplifters. Insurance statistics suggest that perhaps as many as 30 percent of each year's failed businesses go under as a result of employees stealing, ironically destroying the very source of their livelihood.

To deal with this situation, an innovative outfit in New York, calling itself THEFT (an acronym for The Honest Employees Fooling Thieves), places one of its specialists, a young actor, on a site, where he or she works for a while as a typical employee. Then this "employee" gets caught stealing. With lots of screaming and threats, the boss "fires" this person. Normal employees, unaware of the plant, get the message. For a while at least, thefts decline. "Hire Someone to Fire" is the firm's motto.

By Fraud

If possible, those who steal by fraud are even worse than those who steal by force. Embezzlers, swindlers, con artists who exploit the weak are usually the big-time thieves who do the most harm. "The confidence men are the aristocrats of American crime."[1] They're the ones who manipulate things by "rigging contracts, bribing officials, finding loopholes in the tax laws, playing tricks with foreign exchange, lying about the goods we sell and selling trash!"[2]

It's an old, old story. Most of you have heard that in 1624 a Dutchman, Peter Minuit, bought Manhattan Island from Native Americans for $24—which was quite a steal of a deal. But actually the Native Americans who sold Manhattan didn't own it. The sellers were the Canarsees, native to Brooklyn rather than Manhattan. They simply conned Minuit and departed with the loot. The real residents of Manhattan, the Weckquaesgeeks, were just shoved aside. The Canarsees were real businesspeople. They not only sold Manhattan but also sold Staten Island, which wasn't theirs either. And they sold it six times to various groups!

Let's go back even farther. Remember how King Ahab wanted a vineyard near his palace in Jezreel, but the owner, Naboth, refused to sell it, saying, "The LORD forbid that I should give you the inheritance of my fathers" (1 Kings 21:3)? Frustrated, "Ahab went home, sullen and angry," and "lay on his bed sulking and refused to eat. [But then] his wife Jezebel came in and asked him, 'Why are you so sullen? Why won't you eat?'" (vv. 4-5). In response, Ahab told his sad story. Then "Jezebel his wife said, 'Is this how you act as king over Israel? Get up and eat! Cheer up. I'll get you the vineyard of Naboth the Jezreelite'" (v. 7).

So she initiated a plan whereby Naboth was falsely accused and was stoned to death, and Ahab got his vineyard. So the world turns! Kings and queens do things that way. Powerful people, rich people, stock gurus, and con artists scheme, manipulate, and defraud. White-collar crime pervades the business world. Bank robbers usually get a few thousand dollars at best. Insider traders on Wall Street get millions and millions. One man said, "The marketplace is a jungle. The big cats stalk their prey, the jackals lie in wait for the weak, and the rats fight over the leavings." With a strange perversity "The Golden Rule of the world of economics has been distorted to 'Do your neighbor before he does you.'"

Plagiarism

We also steal when we claim other people's poems, songs, and essays and use them as our own. Were we to steal an artist's statue, it would be obvious we had taken something that belongs to him. But when we take a composer's lyrics or a scholar's research or a journalist's story or a preacher's sermon, we're stealing just as much.

One of the most prominent preachers 50 years ago was Harry Emerson Fosdick. One Sunday while on vacation, he went to a small church in Maine and found himself listening to one of his own sermons, delivered by a young pastor who pretended it was his own. Following the message, Fosdick praised the sermon and asked the young man how long it had taken him to prepare it. "About 3 hours," said the young man.

"You're a fast worker," Fosdick replied. "It took me 21 hours."

It's now an industry, this business of plagiarism! In every issue of *Rolling Stone,* a magazine widely read by college age young people, one finds ads that promise first-rate term papers for a fee. Years ago one of my students apparently bought one of these papers. He was one of those guys who came to class about half the time, and what work he did was hardly adequate. But his term paper discussed heavyweight philosophers such as Hegel. And the footnotes were most impressive—even citing lengthy quotations in German! To test his honesty, on the final exam I prepared some individualized questions for this student, asking him to explain some of the terms used so smoothly in the paper and to translate some of the German. He knew nothing about his own citations. And he failed the class. Sometimes we teachers are brighter than we look.

Teachers know cheating occurs. Around a third of high school and college students admit to cheating. When students cheat, of course, they steal from their fellow students who do honest work. Cheating in school and plagiarizing research papers violate the eighth commandment. When we steal a person's words, when we take and use another's ideas, we steal what's in fact most truly his or hers. Even worse, when we steal, we torpedo our own integrity. The damage we do when we cheat most seriously damages our own souls.

NEW TESTAMENT INTERNALIZATION: LIVING HONESTLY BY MAKING AN HONEST LIVING

While running for his party's presidential nomination in 1960, John F. Kennedy visited a coal mine in West Virginia, where he talked with one of the miners. "Is it true you're the son of one of the wealthiest men?" the miner asked. Kennedy admitted he was multimillionaire Joseph Kennedy's son.

"Is it true," the miner continued, "that you've never wanted for anything and had everything you wanted?"

"I guess so," said Kennedy.

"Is it true you've never done a day's work with your hands all your life?" Kennedy nodded yes.

"Well, let me tell you this," said the miner. "You haven't missed a thing."[3]

So it seems to lots of us who earn a living by daily toil. Working often seems a drag, a bore, a necessary evil perhaps, but still nothing to relish. We're a bit like a guy who was asked, "How long you been working here?" and who responded, "Ever since the boss threatened to fire me."

Whether we like it or not, work is important. In fact, it's part of living honestly—making an honest living. When we look for New Testament amplifications on the Old Testament commandment against stealing, we find, amazingly enough, admonitions to work. Paul said, "He who has been stealing must steal no longer, but must work, doing something useful with his own hands, that he may have something to share with those in need" (Ephesians 4:28).

Make Goods That Are Good

Oscar Wilde once said, "Work is the refuge of people who have nothing better to do."[4] Now that's a clever comment, but it's untrue. A bit more realistically, Ogden Nash quipped, "If you don't want to work, you have to work in order to earn enough money so that you won't have to work."[5]

In truth, we've nothing better to do than good work. We work because we need to help meet the world's need for good stuff, the goods we need in order to live well. We should work so as to add good things to our world. As men and women created in God's image, we are creative. We can fashion good stuff that makes our world a better place, more abundant and beautiful.

Unfortunately, one of the negative dividends of the industrial revolution is this: it took from most of us the opportunity to develop our craft skills. When we work in an office punching a computer keyboard or in a factory screwing taps on bolts, we rarely feel creative. We feel as if we're reduced to robots; we become part of a vast machine that is spitting out identical items for mass markets.

Yet we feel, deep in our hearts, that we should do creative work, artistic work. "Originality and the feeling of one's own dignity are achieved only through work and struggle," said one author.[6] Another asserted, "The artist is not a special kind of [person], but every [person] is a special kind of artist."[7] That's so true. Admittedly few of us are Michelangelo-type artists. Most of us have the limited kind of artistic skills that should develop in the work we do.

I'm not a great writer, such as Ernest Hemingway, but as a teacher I need to write as well as I can. I'm no Billy Graham as a preacher, but when preaching I must speak as well as I can. Doing so unleashes whatever artistic talent is latent within me. The world and the world's peoples need the goods that can be made only by workers who work well, doing so with a dedication to live honestly by making an honest living.

Do Good!

Let's turn to another biblical passage. In 2 Thessalonians Paul directed his readers:

In the name of the Lord Jesus Christ, we command you, brothers, to keep away from every brother who is idle and does not live according to the teaching you received from us. For you yourselves know how you ought to follow our example. We were not idle when we were with you, nor did we eat anyone's food without paying for it. On the contrary, we worked night and day, laboring and toiling so that we would not be a burden to any of you. We did this, not because we do not have the right to such help, but in order to make ourselves a model for you to follow. For even when we were with you, we gave you this rule: "If a man will not work, he shall not eat" *(3:6-10)*.

One of the great Christian movements of all time was launched by Benedict in the sixth century. His followers, the Benedictine monks, did much of the missionary-evangelistic work that converted the barbarians, making Europe a Christian place 500 years later. The motto of the Benedictines is this: *Oro et labore*—"Pray and work." To work is to pray. Work well and pray well. Pray well and work well. To be a blessing, to truly bless our world, we must work and pray, pray and work, to the glory of God the Father.

Not only is work good for our own sense of self-

worth, but also work is important because it helps us over-
come our own self-centeredness, our continual tendency to
live only for ourselves. By its very nature, work is a com-
munal endeavor. We build bonds with others by joining together to make things.

I read about a woman who took her son with her to
work one day. She had talked with him about the office before, and when she mentioned the possibility of his spend-
ing a day with her, he seemed genuinely excited. Though
ordinarily shy, he seemed eager to meet each of her coworkers when she introduced them. After a day on the job,
however, he was clearly unhappy. Going home, the mother
asked her son what was troubling him. Finally he opened
up and expressed his disappointment. "I never got to see
the clowns you said you worked with," he complained.[8]

Too often that's our attitude. We see work as a necessary evil, something we do merely to make money, and we
see our coworkers as folks to be tolerated—clearly less
competent than we are. Our incurable self-centeredness
soils our attitudes and behaviors in our workplace.

That's the thrust of Paul's admonition to the Thessalonians: Do your duty! Work to sustain the social bonds we
all need. Doing one's share, contributing to the good of the
whole, is one way to give ourselves away. So not only must
we work ourselves, but also we must insist that others
work. And we must, where possible, devise ways for them
to find work.

I confess that I'm by nature an introvert, a person who
craves solitude, easily content doing things on my own. I
don't particularly need or desire to work together with
other people. I'm temperamentally a long-distance runner
rather than a basketball player. If you have something you
need done, just give me an individual assignment and let
me do it. I think that folks like me have a certain role to
play, a clear niche to fill, in the grand scheme of things.

For this reason it's good for me to work at a college.

Here I must interact with and support faculty colleagues. I must follow the policies established by the administration. I must teach the classes others have decided students need, not simply those I happen to enjoy. I must study, grade papers, and help students learn what they need to learn, not necessarily what appeals to me. I'm not really free to do my own thing as a teacher.

And that's good for my soul, as well as good for my world, for I need to work for others. I contribute, in however small a way, to the good of those around me by working with others for a cause that's bigger than any one of us.

Be Good

We are, of course, regularly reminded of those who are unemployed. President Calvin Coolidge once said, "When more and more people are thrown out of work, unemployment results."[9] Well, yes, how profound! And how awful! Folks need to work to feel they are worthy persons.

More succinctly, Albert Camus declared, "Without work all life goes rotten."[10] So we really don't do anyone a favor by putting him or her on welfare. The Bible clearly urges us to give alms, to share with the needy. But Paul also makes it clear that we should give to people to help them through a crisis, not to free them from working themselves.

That's simply the biblical way. Unlike the ancient Greeks, who rather despised manual labor, the Hebrews always stressed its dignity. "He who does not teach his son a trade," said the rabbis, "teaches him to steal." So Paul, a "Hebrew of Hebrews" (Philippians 3:5), draws upon his own heritage, the Jewish tradition, urging believers (many of them slaves) to work industriously.

Good work gives us dignity. Good work helps us become what we're designed to be. Good work enables us to realize our potential as human beings.

Concert violinists know the difference between a violin and a Stradivarius violin. Centuries ago, Antonio Stradivari simply made the best violins ever made. Stradivari explained his commitment to his task this way:

> When any master holds 'twixt chin and hand a violin of mine, he will be glad that Stradivari lived, made violins, and made them of the best. . . . For while God gives him skill, I give him instruments to play upon, God choosing me to help him. . . . If my hand slacked, I should rob God. . . . He could not make Antonio Stradivari's violins without Antonio.[11]

God, give us more Antonios whose work blesses our world!

Key Scripture: Exodus 20:16

Background Scripture:
Exodus 23:1-3; Proverbs
18:21; Ephesians 4:15;
James 1:26; 3:1-2, 8-10

> *You shall not*
> *give false testi-*
> *mony against*
> *your neighbor.*

CHAPTER 12

THE SANCTITY OF
OUR WORD

OLD TESTAMENT FOUNDATION: NO FALSE WITNESSES

We live in a litigious society. "Litigious" (pronounced luh-TI-jes), if you don't recognize the word, means continually taking others to court, launching lawsuits like arrows to rectify injustices or reclaim elusive "rights."

The story is told of a burglar in California who fell through a skylight while robbing a school. Alleging himself permanently disabled, he sued the school for negligence. A compassionate court apparently felt his pain and awarded him a total of $260,000 in damages, plus a $1,200 monthly stipend. Now that's the kind of crime that pays!

Then there's a woman who claimed to have mysterious psychic powers. She developed some physical ailment, she sought treatment, and the hospital administered a CAT (computerized axial tomography) scan, which involved injecting dye into the brain. As a result, she claims, she lost her psychic powers. Then she successfully sued the hospital and won $1 million in damages.[1] If you think about that a bit, you might question her psychic powers, for surely she could have foreseen the CAT scan risks and refused to allow it.

A British lawyer, F. E. Smith, once cross-examined a man who claimed his arm had been permanently disabled by a bus driver's negligence. Smith first said, "Will you please show us how high you can lift your arm now?" The man struggled, obviously in great pain, unable to raise his arm to shoulder level. "Thank you," said Smith. "Now, would you please show us how high you could raise it before the accident?" Eager to impress the court, the young man fully extended his arm aloft—and, of course, lost his suit in the process.[2]

In all too many such cases there's more at stake than money. What's at stake is truth—truthfulness in court. When folks lie in court, they not only defraud somebody but also subvert one of the best guarantors of a good society—a fair judicial system. All good societies need an honest and equitable legal system.

So with that in mind, let's consider the ninth commandment: "You shall not give false testimony against your neighbor" (Exodus 20:16), or in the KJV translation, "Thou shalt not bear false witness against thy neighbour." If we're to walk with God, if we're to remain in covenant relationship with Him—which is, we must always remember, the purpose of the Ten Commandments, the "10 steps to freedom"—we must never bear false witness against our neighbor, especially in formal, public, or legal ways. What this commandment forbids is clear: deliberate, false, malicious testimony. That's made clear a bit later in Exodus, which says, "Do not spread false reports. Do not help a wicked man by being a malicious witness. Do not follow the crowd in doing wrong. When you give testimony in a lawsuit, do not pervert justice by siding with the crowd, and do not show favoritism to a poor man in his lawsuit" (23:1-3).

We easily understand the importance of truthful witnesses. A wicked man may escape punishment if witnesses lie for him. A good man may be punished if witnesses lie against him. Juries who cave in to public opinion and judges who favor the economically disadvantaged—all cooperate in falsifying the truth, dislodging the balance of justice.

Intent Constitutes a Lie

In the 1960s, when young folks marched in the streets and dreamed of making the world a better place, one of the oft-repeated slogans was, "You can't trust anyone over 30." As the marchers aged, of course, that creed quickly lost its luster!

Another slogan in that era said, "Tell it like it is." That's still a good goal. It's always been so, for it's a reasonably clear definition of truth. I like that motto. It's admirable and worth embracing. I always want to tell it like it is; I want to tell the truth. However, if telling the truth means describing things as they are, with precise details, most of us fail daily. Many of us struggle to tell it like it is exactly. We're less than candid at times, we often err, we disguise the truth to shield others' feelings, and we do in fact fail to state the facts.

Without intending to, I sometimes speak untruths when I speak in chapel! In one message, differentiating the genetic characteristics of the sexes, I claimed that the genetic process that produces a male of our species involves an XY mating with a YY. In fact, I should have said an XX mates with a YY—as one of our biology professors reminded me immediately after chapel. Now I realize that I should be more careful, especially when I'm checking my facts in a reference work. Still, when I'm speaking, my mind too frequently slips some cogs.

In the process of teaching, I sometimes mislead my students with false information and later feel utterly humiliated by my errors. Since I generally have a good memory, and since I think teaching is more than reading prepared scripts for lectures, I seem destined to commit such errors. And truthfully, I fail to tell the full truth in such instances. I feel guilty for such failures, and I duly admit them when necessary. But I don't really intend to err. My obligation to tell the truth is obvious. My ability always to tell it like it is slips and slides as I try my best to do so. Fortunately, for me at least, the ninth commandment has little to do with my inadvertent failures to tell it like it is.

This commandment is not necessarily concerned with whether you say "Fine" or "OK" when I ask, "How ya doin'?" It's not terribly concerned about the scientific accuracy of our efforts to make others feel good when we praise them. It's not concerned with the fact we deceive one another in games and practical jokes. Nor does it insist we abandon rhetorical hyperboles (as Jesus used in many of His parables) designed to elicit a laugh or make a point. In other words, there's lots of latitude in our discourse, and we needn't worry overmuch about always telling it like it is. What we must ever avoid is deliberately telling untruths that harm our neighbors.

No Perjury, No False and Malicious Untruths Allowed

What this commandment forbids is deliberately giving false witness, when the clearly intended testimony is in fact untrue. A contemporary rabbi says, "The Bible is pitiless toward the perjurer. When you stop to think about it, there is probably no more calculatedly vicious crime."[3] In public courtroom testimony, truth must always be told. Still more: even outside the courtroom the Bible forbids slander—the malicious defamation of another.

In an article in the *San Diego Union,* Tom Blair described a scene in a superior court:

Two men were on trial for armed robbery. An eyewitness took the stand, and the prosecutor moved carefully. "So, you say you were on the scene when the robbery took place?"

"Yes," the man said.

"And you saw a vehicle leave at a high rate of speed?"

"Yes."

"And did you observe the occupants?"

"Yes, two men."

"And," the prosecutor boomed, "are those two men present in court today?" At this point, the two defendants sealed their fate. They raised their hands.

Truth to tell, they should have! For in court, folks should tell the truth, even when it hurts. If someone lies in court, it's called perjury—and perjury is a felony. Folks serve hard time in prison for telling lies in court.

Breaking the ninth commandment entails malice—a lie must be malicious, as well as intentional and clearly untrue.

Malicious untruths attack persons. As one author insists, "Deceit and violence—these are the two forms of deliberate assault on human beings."[4]

Italian Dictator Benito Mussolini once said, "Our motto must be to lie in order to conquer."[5] And so he sought to construct his fascist regime, rooted in and riddled with lies.

Like many moderns, Mussolini seemed to inhale some of the ideas of a German philosopher and atheist, Friedrich Nietzsche, who declared, "A great man—what is he? . . . He rather lies than tells the truth; it requires more spirit and will."[6]

Yet when we shatter the trust we need in order to live with one another and we follow Nietzsche's admonition and impose our willed untruths on our world, we destroy it. Lies poison our world. And we're as guilty for poisoning the moral atmosphere as we are for poisoning the air.

Several years ago I had a student who tried to live according to Nietzsche's teaching. In a class where I require reports describing the past week's reading, I noticed a section of his third report that duplicated his second report. Then his fourth report duplicated almost all his third week's report! When I confronted him with this, he wrote a long letter explaining how he could, with effort, imagine how someone like me might imagine he was cheating. But he declared he wasn't, however identical the two reports appeared. His saying so made it so in his mirror-encased private world.

Later he turned in a report claiming to discuss Nietzsche's *Birth of Tragedy*. I suspected that nothing in the report dealt with Nietzsche's book, since the student was waxing eloquent about the kinds of things you find on book jackets. I took the time to read the entire book and confirmed my suspicions. We had an interesting confrontation. At first he claimed he had read the book, but it soon became evident (since he could answer none of my questions) that he knew nothing about it.

Then he shifted his approach, arguing that it didn't matter what he read or even if he had read what he claimed. What mattered was what he thought—and his thoughts, of course, were marvelous. Then he made an astounding claim: looking at the side of a building, he said, "If I see dancing girls on the wall, they're there, whether you see them or not."

Had I thought quickly, I would have pulled out my grade book and said, "Here's your name—you see A, and I see F."

My student deliberately tried to deceive me. He wanted to get a good grade without working. In doing so, he was willing to harm indirectly the students who were doing honest work. In lying, he corrupted the whole academic climate, just as witnesses who lie corrupt the whole judicial climate. And neither can please the Lord!

NEW TESTAMENT INTERNALIZATION: TRUTHFUL TONGUES

Words make our world. Think about it: Words make our world! There's nothing more worthwhile than a word. Nothing's more world-shaping or world-shaking than a word. Nothing's stronger than the tongue. Most parts of the human body slowly atrophy in time. Arthritis and tendinitis assail us older folks, limiting the action of our knees and shoulders. But the tongue stays forever young. The tongue's too strong to wear out, ever.

So when we turn from the Old Testament, where the ninth commandment insists we not bear false witness against our neighbor, to the New Testament, where the law is internalized through the presence of the Lord Jesus by the power of His Holy Spirit, we find a sustained concern that we speak rightly about our neighbor. As Christians, we're called not simply to speak the truth—but to speak "the truth in love" (Ephesians 4:15).

Jesus' brother James, in his powerful little letter, declared, "If anyone considers himself religious and yet does not keep a tight rein on his tongue, he deceives himself and his religion is worthless" (1:26). In the third chapter he picks up the same theme: "Not many of you should presume to be teachers, my brothers, because you know that we who teach will be judged more strictly. We all stumble in many ways. If anyone is never at fault in what he says, he is a perfect man, able to keep his whole body in check" (vv. 1-2).

There's Power to Kill in the Tongue

Continuing, James notes that we can control horses and ships, "but no man can tame the tongue. It is a restless evil, full of deadly poison" (3:8).

When I was young, a child offended or hurt by another's words often chanted, "Sticks and stones may break my bones, but words will never hurt me." It's a statement you still hear on playgrounds. Like many popular sayings, this one expresses a partial truth: sticks and stones really do break bones. But it suggests something utterly untrue in saying words won't hurt, for while sticks and stones may break bones, they break *only* bones, while words may scar forever.

"The tongue has the power of life and death," says Proverbs 18:21. Our words are mightier than machine guns; bullets take lives, destroying bodies, but words penetrate deeper, destroying souls. To modify a childhood taunt, "Sticks and stones may break our bones, but words can shred my soul!"

There's Also Power to Heal with the Tongue

So powerful is it, in fact, that "with the tongue we praise our Lord and Father, and with it we curse men, who have been made in God's likeness. Out of the same mouth come praise and cursing. My brothers, this should not be" (James 3:9-10).

Though we're tempted to dwell on the negative powers of the tongue, we must note there's also power to heal, power in praise. Though the phrases of James largely warn us to avoid doing harm, the underlying intent of the passage is positive. Just as we bless God with our tongue, so we can bless our neighbor in the same way. What a wonderful opportunity each of us has every day literally to make someone's day with our tongue!

We often say, repeating Napoléon's quip, that "a picture's worth a thousand words," thus indicating words' poverty compared with visual images. Again this is partially true, for we certainly learn information better from pictures than words. Napoléon no doubt understood battle plans better by looking at a map than by listening to a corporal's report. When working on a car's engine, I certainly need illustrations, diagrams—even cartoons—that clarify mechanical matters for me.

Yet it's also true that a word may be worth a thousand pictures. No pictures inwardly warm my heart like the words "I love you" on the lips of my wife. No pictures evoke creative insights within my mind that come with the power of words rightly spoken in conversations with friends and students. No pictures touch my soul as do the lyrics of some songs or poems.

We often say, "Actions speak louder than words," or, "What you do speaks so loudly I can't hear a word you say." This is certainly true. Actions are louder, more arresting, more concrete—not necessarily better, not truer. When our actions belie our words, we stand guilty of lying, and our words lose their value.

Yet, truth to tell, words often speak more loudly than actions. Actions may be more visible, may affect us powerfully at the moment, but they do not enter into and inspire and inwardly mold our souls. What you do for me, be it ever so generous and kind, makes my environment more comfortable. But words spoken to me do more than improve my world. Words may be more life-giving and inspiring than actions. Just as oxygen enters my lungs and thence my blood, so words enter into the pulsating circulatory system of my spirit. As I hear and respond to words, they make me who I am.

That truth is evident in the career of Bill Walsh, a successful football coach. Walsh demanded much from his athletes, he acknowledges, but to get men really to perform, he had to motivate them. The best way to motivate football players, he found, was not with threats or bribes. He discovered that "the simplest way to motivate people is plain, old-fashioned praise, handed out in the right way at the right time."[7]

Though money certainly motivates us—and National Football League (NFL) players and coaches are well paid—money's not the most important aspect. Walsh says, "Money talks, but it doesn't always say enough."[8] Positive, powerful words do what money fails to do. Such praise must be precise, properly given, thoroughly truthful. When rightly uttered, words of praise prompt persons to perform in accord with their highest potential.

It's obvious that words are some of the most important realities of our world. We make words, and words make us. It's critical that we use them wisely and well. We reach out and touch and in the process heal with our love. We can bless our world with a touch—and with our words that touch the heart!

Key Scripture: Exodus 20:17

Background Scripture:
Deuteronomy 19:14; 1
Samuel 16:7; Micah 2:1-2;
Matthew 5:3, 8; Luke 12:15;
1 Corinthians 9:24-27;
1 Timothy 6:6-12; 1 John 2:16

*You shall
not covet.*

CHAPTER 13

THE SANCTITY
OF SATISFACTION

OLD TESTAMENT FOUNDATION: DO NOT COVET

When Israel's first king, Saul, backslid and fell from grace, the old prophet Samuel set out to find and anoint his successor. Intent on selecting one of them king, he checked out Jesse's sons, first noting Eliab, the firstborn, who seemed a good prospect. "But the LORD said to Samuel, 'Do not consider his appearance or his height, for I have rejected him. . . . Man looks at the outward appearance, but the LORD looks at the heart'" (1 Samuel 16:7).

God sees the heart! You and I easily evaluate others by their appearance—by the clothes they wear or the color of their hair—but God looks at the heart. We tend to think like Joseph Kennedy, father of a modern political dynasty, who told his kids, "It's not what you are, but what people *think* you are, that really counts" (emphasis added).

For many that's true, for the world generally judges by appearances. "Fake it till you make it" flies well in practice as well as in slogans in many circles. On the contrary, Gregory of Nazianzus, one of the fourth-century church fathers, insisted we embrace this principle: *Esse quam videri*—"We should *be* rather than merely *appear* to be" (emphases added).

Thus, the Ten Commandments, the 10 steps to freedom, begin and end with the heart, the inner self secluded from direct observation. As God's folks, we're offered the prospects of a heart set free. First of all, "You shall have no other gods before me"; second, "You shall not covet." The 10th commandment says, "You shall not covet your neighbor's house. You shall not covet your neighbor's wife, or his manservant or maidservant, his ox or donkey, or anything that belongs to your neighbor" (Exodus 20:17).

The Hebrew word translated "covet" means to "desire, yearn for, lust after" something or someone, seeking self-gratification. It's a strong word, more than mere wishful thinking or daydreaming. The Hebrew word implies taking necessary steps to get what we desire.

Covet No One's House

We're not to covet our neighbor's house. It's healthy and holy to want a house, for to make a home, we need a place to live. We need a house. Most of us know that our family is our most precious earthly society, and a family needs a place in which to live. We need houses—actual physical structures—if we're to make homes, and we need homes in order to live well. Homeless people—dispossessed, rootless, and disrespected—inevitably suffer. There's something simply wrong about being homeless.

So we're right when we seek to secure and protect our homes. My wife and I live in a town house that adequately meets our needs. Over the years she has papered, painted, and redecorated. Her personality is traced in the decor of our home. It's ours; we feel we have certain inalienable rights to it; and we thank the Lord for it. It's OK to want a house, and it's good to own a house.

When I walk to school, however, I see the house of one of my friends, perched on a lofty hillside, with a commanding view of San Diego. His house has more space, a nicer view, and is worth far more than mine. I could begin, while walking to school, to covet his house. Wanting its space, since I've run out of room for my books. Wanting its view, since I like grand vistas. Wanting its resale value, since I want financial security. If I did so, I'd break the 10th commandment. To want for myself what my neighbor owns, to will to get what is his, would be to covet.

That's precisely what happened in ancient Israel 700 years before Christ. As the prophet Micah cried, "Woe to those who plan iniquity, to those who plot evil on their beds! At morning's light they carry it out because it is in their power to do it. They covet fields and seize them, and houses, and take them. They defraud a man of his home, a fellowman of his inheritance" (2:1-2).

That's what's too often happened in America—most visibly when covetous frontier people grabbed the land occupied by various Native American tribes. The year following the 1876 Battle of the Little Bighorn, the Sioux leader Sitting Bull spoke to his people. He told them that "we have now to deal with another race—small and feeble when our fathers first met them but now great and overbearing. Strangely enough, they have a mind to till the soil, and the love of possession is a disease with them."[1] Though not a theologian, not even a Christian, Sitting Bull rightly diagnosed the sin of covetousness, "the love of possession," which was truly a "disease," the desire to get others' houses and lands.

The pioneers' "love of possession" could be clearly seen by indigenous leaders such as Sitting Bull. Less obvious, but equally pernicious, is the class envy that flourishes in today's political climate and tramples on private property rights. Zealous advocates of the "social gospel," self-styled prophets of "social justice," easily slip into confiscating private property, which is the very good protected by the 10th commandment! They're more than willing to "move" their "neighbor's boundary stone" (Deuteronomy 19:14), just as long as they're taking from the rich to grant entitlements to the poor.

A variety of political leaders have appealed to those who have little, promising to give them money or lands that they seize through legislative or bureaucratic means. With his usual insight, Aristotle wrote in *Politics*, centuries before Christ:

> Such legislation [taking private property] may have a specious appearance of benevolence; men readily listen to it, and are easily induced to believe that in some wonderful manner everybody will become everybody's friend, especially when someone is heard denouncing the evils now existing in states, . . . which are said to arise out of the possession of private property. These evils, however, are due to a very different cause—the wickedness of human nature.[2]

To live under the rule of law, securely controlling one's property, truly liberates a person and helps establish the good life. Real freedom, as Friedrich A. Hayek declared, is "always freedom under the law."[3] In his classic economic work, *The Road to Serfdom*, Hayek wrote, "The Rule of Law . . . implies limits to the scope of legislation," forbidding laws "aimed at particular people or at enabling anybody to use the coercive power of the state" to secure personal or class gains.[4]

Don't Covet Others' Spouses and Servants

Not only must we not covet houses and lands, but also we must not covet the persons who make up our neighbor's household. The text says, "You shall not covet your neighbor's wife" (Exodus 20:17). In part, this means we must not entertain lustful, adulterous desires for our neighbor's husband or wife.

Since technology has largely replaced household servants, the literal meaning of part of this commandment cannot be pressed too far. There are, of course, rich folks who employ servants—gardeners, maids. When I ride the San Diego city bus, I'm often surrounded by women who commute from Tijuana, Mexico, to work in wealthy San Diegans' homes. I could envy the wealthy people who can afford servants.

Yet, even if we have no human servants, we are tempted to covet the mechanical "servants" others have. There are tools that make life easier, household appliances that add comfort and validate affluence, machines that literally harness the power of hundreds of horses, which we easily covet. Keeping up with the Joneses exhausts our energies and ingenuity when the Jones family seems forever able to buy the latest gizmo.

Don't Covet Others' Power for Work and Transport

Next, we're told not to covet our neighbor's ox or donkey. In the ancient world, oxen pulled plows—they were the sources of power, the means whereby one prospered. To own lots of oxen enabled one to plow lots of land and make lots of money. So it was easy, especially if one had no oxen at all, to covet a neighbor's livestock.

To be honest with you, I've never been tempted to covet an ox. I couldn't care for one if I owned it. But I'm tempted to covet the power sources that enable folks in our society to succeed. I'm tempted to covet the job, the position, the office of those who appear to be more successful than I.

We all need to work. That's just part of being human. And it's fine to try to find the best job, the work that's right for us. It's fine to want to improve ourselves by working hard and getting even better jobs. It's not covetous to want to do well, to succeed, to advance in our vocation. To attain that end, we obviously need tools such as education, skilled ways to do well.

What's wrong is scheming to get the position, the office, the authority held by another person. At the college where I work, I have a dual position: professor and chaplain. As a professor, it's fine for me to want to do my best, to move up the promotional track from assistant professor to associate professor to full professor. But if I think my department chairman has more influence and authority than I have, and if I want to get his position, I'd be guilty of covetousness. If I wanted to get the academic dean's position, I'd be coveting. If I wanted to become president of the college and hatched plots to dislodge the present president, I'd be covetous. The Bible simply tells me to be content with what I have, to do my best with what's been given me, to work hard and try to succeed but not to succeed at others' expense or loss.

Finally, "You shall not covet your neighbor's . . . donkey." Again, I've never seen a donkey I've wanted. You give me a donkey, and I'll try to give it away as soon as possible! But in the ancient world, of course, donkeys were sturdy transportation vehicles. They served as cars and trucks.

So, to contextualize the commandment: "You shall not desire to get your neighbor's automobile." Most clearly, of course, this means we're not to dream up schemes to steal cars. But, short of that, we're not to resent not having what others have. Automobile advertisements, of course, encourage us to feel we're somehow inadequate as human beings if we're not driving a sleek, low-mileage machine.

There's a standard joke on university campuses pointing out the difference between cars parked in faculty parking lots and those in student lots. Professors often drive beat-up, old economy models, while students seem able to afford expensive ones. Sometimes, however, the jokes disguise a certain resentment, a covetousness, which is wrong. We teachers have willingly embraced a profession whose rewards are not primarily monetary. To envy those whose work delivers greater financial dividends—our students' parents and, in time, many of our students themselves—makes us covetous.

The central truth of the 10th commandment can be discerned in a story Tolstoy told a century ago. There was a certain Russian peasant who, as most peasants do, wanted more land so as to make a better living for himself and his family. As luck would have it, one day a wealthy landowner offered the peasant a deal to beat all deals—he could have all the land he could walk around in a day.

At the break of dawn on the assigned day, the peasant began walking. He had calculated a reasonable amount of land to encircle, but as he walked, his vision expanded. Thus, as he tried to make it back to the starting point by nightfall, he found himself both tired and needing to exert even more energy to make it. With great difficulty, he strained and strained, jogging as well as walking, and just barely made it back in time. At the moment he finished, however, his heart failed, and he fell dead on the land he had just claimed![5] That's covetousness—wanting more than we need, killing ourselves to possess what we have no right to own.

How truly the old German proverb summed it up: "Charity gives itself rich; covetousness hoards itself poor."

NEW TESTAMENT INTERNALIZATION: SIMPLICITY— WHEN ALL YOU'VE EVER WANTED ISN'T ENOUGH

One witty speaker corrupted a familiar scripture: "It's not the *love* of money that's the root of all evil; it's the *lack* of money that's the root of all evil!"

That theme shone through a speech that noted Wall Street financier Ivan Boesky made at the University of California, Berkeley, speaking at the School of Business commencement ceremony. He said, "Greed is good. I want you to know greed is healthy. You can be greedy and feel good about it."[6] At that good news, "the gospel á la Boesky," the budding MBAs and entrepreneurs laughed and applauded.

Boesky's praise of greed, however, seems strangely ironic in view of his subsequent conviction for stealing $300 million through financial fraud. He was in time brought to trial, found guilty, and imprisoned. I wonder if, after paying $50 million in fines, repaying $50 million to investors, and doing time in prison, Boesky sustained the same enthusiasm for the goodness of greed. I wonder if "you can be greedy and feel good about it" in prison.

John the apostle warned against the "lust of [one's] eyes" (1 John 2:16), the infinite, avaricious desire we men and women have to accumulate possessions, especially money. The Old Testament's warning against covetousness, set forth in the 10th commandment, is deepened in the New Testament to a warning against unlimited desires.

Money Draws Us

In Paul's first letter to Timothy we find a passage that follows a warning against those who pervert the way of Jesus into a "success gospel":

> People who want to get rich fall into temptation and a trap and into many foolish and harmful desires that plunge men into ruin and destruction. For the love of money is a root of all kinds of evil. Some people, eager for money, have wandered from the faith and pierced themselves with many griefs (6:9-10).

Like an enormous electromagnet, money tugs continuously at a tiny bit of shrapnel buried deep within each of our hearts. Its pervasive power indwells popular expressions: "Another day, another dollar," indicating money gives meaning to the day. "You get what you pay for," suggesting the worth of goods and services can be reduced to dollars and cents. "The almighty dollar," indicating it is omnipotent. Most of us agree with Richard Armour, who said, "That money talks I'll not deny; I heard it once—it said good-bye!"[7]

Whereas ancient heroes were admired for their courage and medieval heroes were venerated for their sanctity, modern heroes are vaunted for making money—lots of money! Michael Jordan gets an annual eight-figure income for playing basketball. Michael Jackson signs multibillion-dollar contracts for his musical talents. Heavyweight boxing champions get millions for pounding on their opponents for a few minutes. Even the guys who get pounded get millions for their pain!

We easily assume the importance of money, its almost sacred quality, because we live in a world that has routinely been structured by the notion that a man's life and a woman's worth "consist in the abundance of . . . possessions" (Luke 12:15). At times we're tempted to think our consumer society has introduced a totally new issue into the current of our moral life, that never before has money been such a powerful compulsion.

We find, however, when we read the Bible, that it's an ancient issue. Some things rarely change. As sinful men and women, our gods forever remain avarice and greed. Gluttons may want too much food, but they usually reach a limit of consumption. But there's no limit to the amount of money we can deposit in the bank. So money looks infinitely desirable.

Just as the human eye can literally take in the universe, so the human heart endlessly craves more and more money. John D. Rockefeller was once asked how much money he needed to be content. He answered, "Just a little bit more." We're drawn to it. We're deceived into thinking a little more money will finally fulfill us, finally make us what we long to be—happy.

Money Damns Us

That temptation proves fatal, our text insists. Wanting

to get rich is a temptation, a trap, which leads to ruin and destruction. Rockefeller himself, after getting considerably more than a "little bit more," lamented, "I have made many millions, but they have brought me no happiness. I would barter them all for the days I sat on an office stool in Cleveland and counted myself rich on three dollars a week."[8]

Admittedly, wealth has its comforts. One must never argue that the poor are automatically more content with life than the rich. Still it's clear that money by itself doesn't make folks happy. Those who have most loved and singularly pursued money often testify to its vanity.

What the love of money does to us is separate us from God, displacing Him as the focus of our love. Thus, one writer said, "You lack simplicity when you are far from God."[9] That's true, basically, because Jesus said, "Blessed are the pure in heart, for they will see God" (Matthew 5:8). When our vision is clouded by possessions, we fail to see God.

Far from God, we fail to find happiness, for real happiness comes only when we're rightly related to Him. Simplicity sees through the tarnish of the vanity of things to treasure the truths of the mind, the beauty of the imagination, the joys of the heart. Money damns us, not because it's intrinsically evil, but because it diverts us from our true vocation in life—loving God.

Simplicity Frees Us

In Paul's judgment, "godliness with contentment is great gain. For we brought nothing into the world, and we can take nothing out of it. But if we have food and clothing, we will be content with that" (1 Timothy 6:6-8). To deal with money, many spiritual masters urge us to embrace the second "evangelical counsel," poverty. Since that sounds too radical for many of us, we may, I think, more rightly define it as the contentment that flourishes when we resolve to live simply.

It's obvious that many of us live simply, simply because we have to, not because we want to. But the simplicity that contributes to godliness, the simplicity that contents us, is something deliberately embraced. Simplicity is an inward commitment to live free of money's compulsions, free to follow the will of our Lord.

Simplicity—that's the key to contentment. Rather like beginning an exercise program if we want to lose weight, simplifying life is the necessary step to move toward our divinely appointed end, which is the joy that passes understanding.

To simplify our lives is a great art. We need it. Others need it. Planet Earth needs it. Simplicity cleanses our vision to see reality. It helps us see how we ought to live, to see what kinds of persons we ought to be. What we ought to be our text tells us: godly men and women.

So Run! Fight! Hold On!

To live simply, Paul tells us, takes resolve: "But you . . . flee from all this, and pursue righteousness, godliness, faith, love, endurance and gentleness. Fight the good fight of the faith. Take hold of the eternal life to which you were called when you made your good confession in the presence of many witnesses" (1 Timothy 6:11-12).

Note the verbs in these verses: "flee," "pursue," "fight," "take hold." All denote singleness of purpose, simplicity of action. Like athletes laying aside all that would hinder their performance, like soldiers laying aside their packs in the midst of the battle, believers must simplify their lives in order to be at their best for their Lord.

William James wrote, "Athletes are secular saints, and saints are athletes of God." I'm not a great athlete, but I do enjoy running and run road races when I can. One of the positive things about running is it reduces things to a minimum. I need some good shoes, and that's about it.

When I race, I don't carry my suitcase. A lot of women

beat me in the races I run, but not one of them has ever finished ahead of me carrying her purse. Nor have I ever seen a serious male runner with a billfold in his rear pocket. When I line up at the start of a race with a guy who has a Walkman glued to his ears, I know he's no threat. Folks may dance to music, but they win no races.

So it is in the race of life. To run well, we must lay aside all the stuff that hinders us. And when we do so and run well, there's incredible satisfaction. I can't really explain why aging athletes like me pay good money as entry fees to run races we'll never win. But I do know that when I've trained for a race, and when I run my best—especially when I establish a personal record—I just feel right with the world.

Paul summed it up this way:

> Do you not know that in a race all the runners run, but only one gets the prize? Run in such a way as to get the prize. Everyone who competes in the games goes into strict training. They do it to get a crown that will not last; but we do it to get a crown that will last forever. Therefore I do not run like a man running aimlessly; I do not fight like a man beating the air. No, I beat my body and make it my slave so that after I have preached to others, I myself will not be disqualified for the prize (1 Corinthians 9:24-27).

Paul's truth recently dawned on one of America's richest men. In response to a "spiritual reawakening" triggered by disillusionment with his vast collection of possessions, Thomas Monaghan, the founder of Domino's Pizza, suddenly began selling off many of his prized possessions, including three houses designed by Frank Lloyd Wright and 30 vintage automobiles, one a $13 million Bugatti. Construction was halted on his new $5 million home, and there was even talk of selling his Detroit Tigers baseball team if he found it to be "a source of excessive pride." He was quoted as saying, "None of the things I've bought, and I mean none of them, has ever really made me happy."[10]

Yet the Lord would like us to be happy—happy in the blessed sense of the Lord Jesus' beatitudes. Jesus Christ began that list of "blessed" characteristics with the words "Blessed are the poor in spirit" (Matthew 5:3). That, in part, is the spirit that eschews covetousness, the person who is happy to say, "Enough's enough."

NOTES

Chapter 1

1. William Murchison, *Reclaiming Morality in America* (Nashville: Thomas Nelson, 1994), 1.

2. Ibid., 55.

3. Ibid., 86.

4. James Patterson and Peter Kim, *The Day America Told the Truth: What People Really Believe About Everything That Really Matters* (New York: Prentice Hall Press, 1991), 41.

5. Allan Bloom, *The Closing of the American Mind* (New York: Simon and Schuster, 1987), 19-21.

6. Ernest Hemingway, *Death in the Afternoon* (New York: Scribners, 1932), 4.

7. Bloom, *Closing of the American Mind*, 141.

8. *First Things* 45 (August-September 1994): 20-21.

9. William Murchison, *Reclaiming Morality in America*, 53.

10. Manis Friedman, *Doesn't Anyone Blush Anymore? Reclaiming Intimacy, Modesty, and Sexuality in a Permissive Age* (San Francisco: Harper, 1990).

11. Daniel Smith-Rowsey, "The Terrible Twenties," *Newsweek*, June 17, 1991, unnumbered page.

12. Robert H. Schuller, *Believe in the God Who Believes in You* (New York: Bantam Books, 1991), 93-94.

13. John Paul II, *The Splendor of Truth—Veritatus Splendor* (Boston: St. Paul Books and Media, 1993), 104.

14. Ibid., 125.

Chapter 2

1. Rhoda T. Tripp, comp., *The International Thesaurus of Quotations,* (New York: Thomas V. Crowell, Publisher, 1970), 986.

2. "Living by Vows," *Christianity Today*, October 8, 1990, 38-40.

Chapter 3

1. These phrases resonate with lines in T. S. Eliot's "The Love Song of J. Alfred Prufrock," in *The Complete Poems and Plays* (New York: Harcourt, Brace and World, 1962), 4-7.

2. "Life in These United States," *Reader's Digest*, October 1987, 170.

3. The author made a considerable effort to locate the source for

this and other undocumented quotations and illustrations. Appropriate credit, if known, will be included in any reprinting.

Chapter 4

1. Philip Johnson, *Darwin on Trial* (Downers Grove, Ill.: InterVarsity Press, 1991), 114.

2. Ibid., 130.

3. Michael E. Jones, *Desperate Moderns: Modernity as Rationalized Sexual Misbehavior* (San Francisco: Ignatius Press, 1993), 12.

4. Ibid., 181.

5. John Wooden, *They Call Me Coach* (Waco, Tex.: Word Books, 1973), 1.

6. Clifton Fadiman, ed., *The Little Brown Book of Anecdotes* (Boston: Little, Brown and Co., 1985), 15.

7. C. S. Lewis, *Surprised by Joy* (New York: Harcourt Brace, 1955), 228.

8. Nat Shapiro, ed., *Whatever It Is, I'm Against It* (New York: Simon and Shuster, 1984), 265-66.

9. Fadiman, *Little Brown Book of Anecdotes*, 439.

Chapter 5

1. Frank S. Mead, ed., *The Encyclopedia of Religious Quotations* (Westwood, N.J.: Fleming H. Revell, 1965), 243.

2. Ernesto Cardinal, *To Live Is to Love* (New York: Herder and Herder, 1972), 101.

3. Tony Campolo, *The Success Fantasy* (Wheaton, Ill.: Victor Books, 1980), 12.

4. L. S. Stavrianos, *The Promise of the Coming Dark Ages* (San Francisco: W. H. Freeman, 1976), 40.

5. Frederick Dale Bruner, *The Christbook* (Waco, Tex.: Word Books, 1987), 264.

6. Ibid.

7. Ibid.

8. Arthur Schopenhauer in W. H. Auden, *A Certain World* (New York: Viking Press, 1970), 266.

9. Jacques Ellul, *Money and Power* (Downers Grove, Ill.: InterVarsity Press, 1984), 75.

10. Patterson and Kim, *Day America Told the Truth*, 65-66.

11. *McCall's*, September 1990, 57.

12. Ellul, *Money and Power*, 76.

13. John Kenneth Galbraith, *Money* (Boston: Houghton Mifflin, 1975), 4.

14. Paul Lee Tan, *Encyclopedia of 7,700 Illustrations* (Rockville, Md.: Assurance Publishers, 1984), 288-89.

15. William Barclay, *The Gospel of Matthew*, 2nd ed. (Philadelphia: Westminster Press, 1958), 1:244.

16. Ibid.

Chapter 6

1. R. H. Charles, *The Decalogue* (Edinburgh: T. and T. Clark, 1923), 89.

2. Joy Davidman, *Smoke on the Mountain: An Interpretation of the Ten Commandments* (Philadelphia: Westminster Press, 1954), 42-43.

3. Ibid., 43.

4. Randal Earl Denny, *Tables of Stone for Modern Living* (Kansas City: Beacon Hill Press of Kansas City, 1970), 31.

5. *Leadership,* summer 1991, 110-14.

6. Fadiman, *Little Brown Book of Anecdotes,* 555.

7. William Lambdin, *Doublespeak Dictionary* (Los Angeles: Pinnacle Books, 1979), 98.

8. Bruner, *Christbook,* 202.

Chapter 7

1. Abraham Joshua Heschel, *The Sabbath: Its Meaning for Modern Man* (New York: Farrar, Straus and Giroux, 1951), 3-4.

2. Jörgen Moltmann, *God in Creation* (San Francisco: Harper and Row, 1985), 280.

3. C. S. Lewis, "Historicism," in *Christian Reflections* (Grand Rapids, Mich.: William B. Eerdmans, 1967), 113.

4. James Houston, *I Believe in the Creator* (Grand Rapids, Mich.: William B. Eerdmans, 1980), 162.

5. From *To the Magnesians,* 9.

6. Charles, *Decalogue,* 139.

Chapter 8

1. Dr. Dobson told this story when he spoke at MidAmerica Nazarene College in Olathe, Kansas, when I was on the faculty in the 1970s.

2. Napoléon Bonaparte, *Maxims* (1804-15), quoted in Tripp, *International Thesaurus of Quotations,* 141.

3. Dietrich Bonhoeffer, *A Testament of Freedom* (New York: Harper Collins, 1990), 53.

4. Ibid., 109.

5. Ibid., 537.

6. Tripp, *International Thesaurus of Quotations,* 248.

7. Bruner, *Christbook,* 393.

8. Sidney Ahlstrom, *A Religious History of the American People* (New Haven, Conn.: Yale University Press, 1932), 864-65.

Chapter 9

1. Bruner, *Christbook,* 175.

2. Fadiman, *Little Brown Book of Anecdotes,* 422.

3. Ibid., 298.

4. Ibid., 32.

5. Ibid., 47.

Chapter 10

1. *Time,* June 23, 1967.

2. Patterson and Kim, *Day America Told the Truth,* 94-99.

3. Ibid., 96.

4. Fadiman, *Little Brown Book of Anecdotes,* 227.

5. Albert Camus, *The Fall* (1957), quoted in Robert Byrne, *1,911 Best Things Anybody Ever Said* (New York: Fawcett Columbine, 1988), 113.

6. A December 1991 article in *McCall's* stresses that personal intimacy is one of the "five dimensions" of healthy marriages, far more important than sexual performance.

7. Josh McDowell, *Why Wait?* (Waco, Tex.: Word Publishing, 1994), 125.

8. Friedman, *Doesn't Anyone Blush Anymore?* 64.

Chapter 11

1. Davidman, *Smoke on the Mountain,* 97.

2. Ibid., 97-98.

3. Fadiman, *Little Brown Book of Anecdotes,* 327.

4. Lawrence J. Peter, *Peter's Quotations* (New York: Bantam Books, 1979), 535.

5. Ibid.

6. Fyodor Dostoyevsky, *A Diary of a Writer* (1873), quoted in Tripp, *International Thesaurus of Quotations,* 107.

7. Eric Gill, *A Holy Tradition of Working: An Anthology of the Writing of Eric Gill* (West Stockbridge, Mass.: Lindisfarne Press, 1983), 58.

8. Marvella McDill, contributor to "All in a Day's Work," *Reader's Digest,* October 1988, 121.

9. "Immortal Remark," *New York Herald Tribune,* September 29, 1954, in George Seldes, *The Great Quotations* (New York: Pocket Books, 1967), 986.

10. Peter, *Peter's Quotations,* 537.

11. Harry Emerson Fosdick, *The Meaning of Prayer* (New York: Abingdon Press, 1915), 64.

Chapter 12

1. Chuck Colson, *A Dance with Deception* (Dallas: Word Publishing, 1993), 70.

2. Fadiman, *Little Brown Book of Anecdotes,* 513.

3. Robert I. Kahn, *The Letter and the Spirit* (Waco, Tex.: Word Books, 1972), 70.

4. Sissela Bok, *Lying: Moral Choice in Public and Private Life* (New York: Vintage Books, 1978), 19.

5. Benito Mussolini, "Instructions to Fernando Mezzasoma," in Seldes, *Great Quotations*, 607.

6. Friedrich Nietzsche, *The Will to Power*, quoted in Bok, *Lying*, 18.

7. Bill Walsh, "The Case for Kudos," *Forbes ASAP*, October 1994, 17.

8. Ibid.

Chapter 13

1. T. C. McLuhan, *Touch the Earth* (New York: Pocket Books, 1972), 90.

2. Aristotle, *Politics 2.5*, trans. Benjamin Jowett.

3. Gottfried Dietze, "Hayek on the Rule of Law," in *Essays on Hayek*, ed. Fritz Machlup (Hillsdale, Mich.: Hillsdale College Press, 1976), 110.

4. Friedrich A. Hayek, *The Road to Serfdom* (Chicago: Phoenix Books, 1944), 83-84.

5. Denny, *Tables of Stone for Modern Living*, 111.

6. Quoted by Richard Halverson, chaplain of the United States Senate (address given at Conference on Biblical Exposition, Anaheim, Calif., 1985).

7. Peter, *Peter's Quotations*, 346.

8. Tan, *Encyclopedia of 7,700 Illustrations*, 827.

9. Raissa Maritain, *We Have Been Friends Together* (Garden City, N.Y.: Image Books, 1961), 136.

10. Thomas H. Naylor, "The Living Dead," *New Oxford Review* 59, No. 4 (September 1992): 26.

RESOURCES FOR FURTHER READING

To read the author's full version from which this Dialog book has been adapted, see Gerard Reed, *The Liberating Law* (Kansas City: Beacon Hill Press of Kansas City, 1996).

Barclay, William. *The Old Law and the New Law*. Philadelphia: Westminster Press, 1972.

_____. *The Ten Commandments for Today*. San Francisco: Harper San Francisco, 1973.

Bonhoeffer, Dietrich. *The Cost of Discipleship*. Rev. ed. New York: Macmillan Co., 1963.

Brooks, Roger. *The Spirit of the Ten Commandments: Shattering the Myth of Rabbinic Legalism*. San Francisco: Harper and Row, 1990.

Chappell, Clovis. *Ten Rules for Living*. Nashville: Abingdon, 1966.

Charles, R. H. *The Decalogue*. Edinburgh: T. and T. Clark, 1923.

Davidman, Joy. *Smoke on the Mountain: An Interpretation of the Ten Commandments*. Philadelphia: Westminster Press, 1954.

Denny, Randal Earl. *Tables of Stone for Modern Living*. Kansas City: Beacon Hill Press of Kansas City, 1970.

Harrelson, Walter J. *The Ten Commandments and Human Rights*. Philadelphia: Fortress Press, 1980.

Heschel, Abraham Joshua. *God in Search of Man: A Philosophy of Judaism*. New York: Farrar, Strauss, and Giroux, 1955.

_____. *The Sabbath: Its Meaning for Modern Man*. New York: Farrar, Strauss, and Giroux, 1951.

Kahn, Robert I. *The Letter and the Spirit*. Waco, Tex.: Word Books, 1972.

Killinger, John. *To My People with Love: The Ten Commandments for Today*. Nashville: Abingdon Press, 1988.

Lewis, C. S. *The Abolition of Man*. New York: Macmillan Co., 1947.

_____. *Christian Reflections*. Grand Rapids, Mich.: William B. Eerdmans, 1967.

_____. *Mere Christianity*. New York: Macmillan Co., 1952.

Schuller, Robert H. *Believe in the God Who Believes in You*. New York: Bantam Books, 1991.

Seamands, David A. *God's Blueprint for Living: New Perspectives on the Ten Commandments*. Wilmore, Ky.: Bristol Books, 1988.

Smedes, Lewis B. *Mere Morality: What God Expects from Ordinary People*. Grand Rapids, Mich.: William B. Eerdmans, 1983.

Trueblood, Elton. *Foundations for Reconstruction*. New York: Harper and Brothers, 1946.

Williams, Jay G. *Ten Words of Freedom*. Philadelphia: Fortress Press, 1971.